SCRAP YOUR *real* LIFE

by kristin rutten

*Dedicated to the following contributing artists, whose
storytelling & scrapbooking talents brought these ideas to life...*

Terry Billman

Barbara Clayton

Jennifer DeLorenzo

Jennifer Fox

Michelle Godin

Kelly-Ann Halbert

Eryn Herbert

Rebecca Kuchenbecker

Dawn McFarland

Crystal Livesay

Kimberly Lund

Valerie Pfeffer

Alisa Schenck

Jessica Bree Thompson

Stacey Truman

Creative Outlet Publishing
418 East Broadway
Lewistown, MT 59457
www.CreativeOutletPublishing.com

CONTENTS

Introduction   4

Scrap Your Real Life in 5 Simple Steps   5

Theme One: The Jobs We Do   7

Theme Two: The Ways We Connect   25

Theme Three: The Ways We Get Around   43

Theme Four: The Foods We Eat   59

Theme Five: Our Personal Style   75

Theme Six: The Ways We Entertain   91

Theme Seven: The Ways We Shop & Do Business   107

Theme Eight: The Ways We Are Challenged   123

Contributor Index   139

INTRODUCTION

Have you ever run out of topics to scrap about? You want to capture your everyday life but can't get inspired because your day-to-day existence seems so routine, so mundane, that you can't imagine why anyone would ever want to hear more about it, let alone take the time to scrapbook it.

Or perhaps there are so many stories you'd like to share you fear you'll never get them all done. If this is you, chances are your photos are piling up faster than you can scrap them, you can't seem to get around to keeping a daily journal, and you feel a lot of guilt connected to this activity that's supposed to be fun.

Maybe you're just starting to wonder if the pages you are creating are telling the stories you truly want to tell ... the ones your family and friends will most cherish years down the road.

If any of these scenarios describes your situation, it may be time to take a step back and think a bit more about your approach to memory keeping. A little thought and a bit more focus can go a long way toward helping you create scrapbooks you and those you love will truly treasure, while at the same time bringing back the joy you felt when you first discovered this amazing hobby.

Scrap Your Real Life is here to help you find that focus. In the next eight chapters, you'll find thought-provoking questions, journaling prompts, photo ideas, suggested scrapbooking approaches and sample layouts all centered around specifically chosen themes designed to help you capture your everyday real life. Each of those themes is broken into five simple steps, as depicted in the image on the right, and presented in a workbook-style format to guide you through the process.

A key component to this approach is the practice of thinking beyond the present moment when considering the memories you'd like to document. Specifically, you are asked to take a look at those who came before you and ask yourself... what information, photos and stories do I wish I had from those times? You are also invited to imagine future readers of your scrapbooks and consider how life may have changed by the time they find your page. This will help you identify the parts of today's experience that may later be especially interesting to hear more about.

This book was designed to help kick-start your thought process, focus in on what's most interesting about your everyday life and inspire your journey toward creating meaningful scrapbook pages.

Now... get ready to scrap your real life!

> A little thought and a bit more focus can go a long way toward helping you create scrapbooks you and those you love will truly treasure...

WHO might like to hear about this part of your life?

How could sharing this **BENEFIT** you or others?

If you don't share this, **WHO WILL**?

SCRAP YOUR *real* LIFE
in 5 easy steps

STEP ① IDENTIFY YOUR WHY

Clarify why & for whom the topic may be meaningful.

What **STORIES**, experiences or memories would you like to share on this topic?

STEP ② BRAINSTORM STORY IDEAS

Use questions & journaling prompts to explore stories related to this topic area.

What **PHOTOS** & **ITEMS** do you already have?

What is **MISSING**?

What do you **WISH** you had from earlier times?

STEP ③ GET THE WHOLE PICTURE

Take a look at the photos & memorabilia you have ... or wish you had ... to help tell this story.

Check out the work of others on this topic, such as scrapbook **layouts**, **mini-albums**, favorite **quotations** or other resources.

STEP ④ BE INSPIRED

Explore how others have shared similar stories to spark ideas of your own.

What **MATERIALS** would fit well with this topic area?

What **DESIGN** ideas might be fun to try when telling this story?

STEP ⑤ PULL IT ALL TOGETHER

Gather up your answers, ideas & inspiration and have fun scrapping your real life!

SCRAP YOUR *real* LIFE
.com

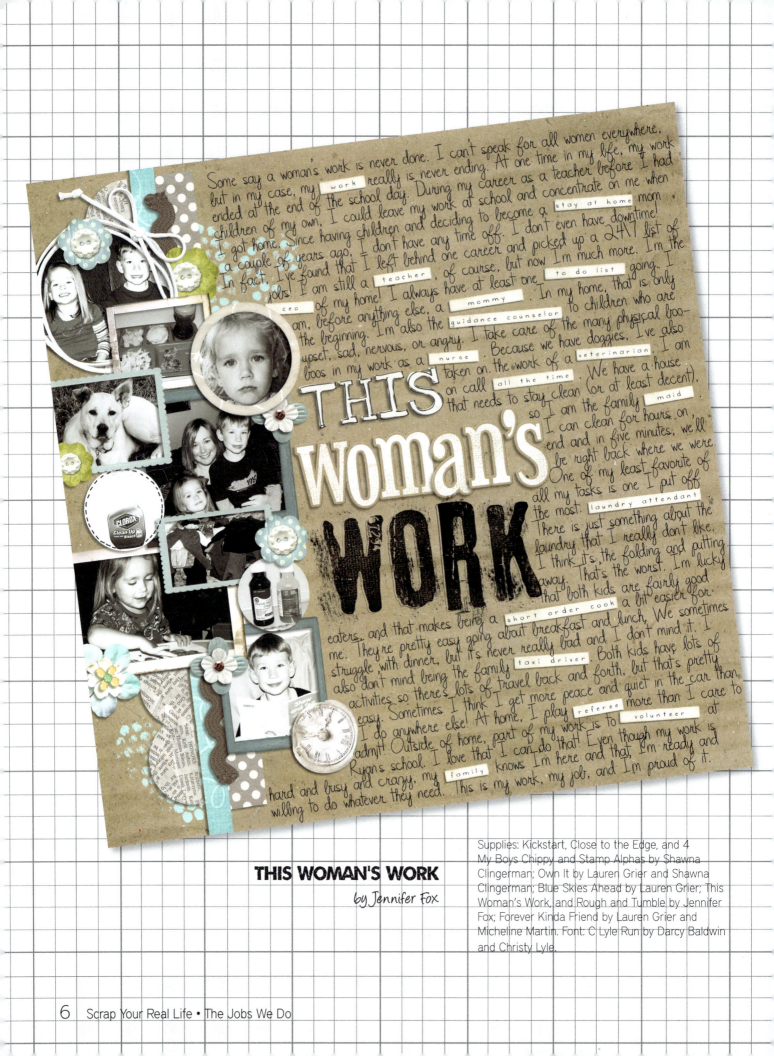

Some say a woman's work is never done. I can't speak for all women everywhere, but in my case, my `work` really is never ending. At one time in my life, my work ended at the end of the school day. During my career as a teacher before I had children of my own, I could leave my work at school and concentrate on me when I got home. Since having children and deciding to become a `stay at home` mom a couple of years ago, I don't have any time off. I don't even have downtime! In fact, I've found that I left behind one career and picked up a 24\7 list of jobs. I am still a `teacher`, of course, but now I'm much more. I'm the `ceo` of my home! I always have at least one `to do list` going. I am, before anything else, a `mommy`. In my home, that is only the beginning. I'm also the `guidance counselor` to children who are upset, sad, nervous, or angry. I take care of the many physical boo-boos in my work as a `nurse`. Because we have doggies, I've also taken on the work of a `veterinarian`. I am on call `all the time`. We have a house that needs to stay clean (or at least decent), so I am the family `maid`. I can clean for hours on end and in five minutes, we'll be right back where we were. One of my least favorite of all my tasks is one I put off the most. `laundry attendant` There is just something about the laundry that I really don't like. I think it's the folding and putting away. That's the worst. I'm lucky that both kids are fairly good eaters, and that makes being a `short order cook` a bit easier for me. They're pretty easy going about breakfast and lunch. We sometimes struggle with dinner, but it's never really bad and I don't mind it. I also don't mind being the family `taxi driver`. Both kids have lots of activities so there's lots of travel back and forth, but that's pretty easy. Sometimes I think I get more peace and quiet in the car than I do anywhere else! At home, I play `referee` more than I care to admit. Outside of home, part of my work is to `volunteer` at Ryan's school. I love that I can do that. Even though my work is hard and busy and crazy, my `family` knows I'm here and that, I'm ready and willing to do whatever they need. This is my work, my job, and I'm proud of it.

THIS WOMAN'S WORK

by Jennifer Fox

Supplies: Kickstart, Close to the Edge, and 4 My Boys Chippy and Stamp Alphas by Shawna Clingerman; Own It by Lauren Grier and Shawna Clingerman; Blue Skies Ahead by Lauren Grier; This Woman's Work, and Rough and Tumble by Jennifer Fox; Forever Kinda Friend by Lauren Grier and Micheline Martin. Font: C Lyle Run by Darcy Baldwin and Christy Lyle.

THEME ONE

THE JOBS WE DO

Goal:
Create a scrapbook page that provides insight into the role your job, career or occupation plays in your daily life at this point in time.

The work you do reveals a wealth of information about you. Your "job" may be a traditional paid occupation or you may spend your days as a stay-at-home parent. You may volunteer your time for the good of your community or juggle multiple roles. Perhaps you have retired from professional work and entered a new stage of life.

Whether you spend your days toiling at a job you hate just to make ends meet or find great satisfaction in the career of your dreams, your occupation says a lot about your priorities and values, your interests, your talents and skills, even your background.

The story of your work goes even further, however, and helps paint a picture of the world where you live ... the economic climate, social norms, technological advances, and so much more.

LEARN
by Kelly-Ann Halbert

I love my job as a trainer but there's always some niggling at me whenever I teach. I always fear that I'll look like a fraud/child as a teacher of adult students. Would find out about my own Education. How would these people with degrees react if they knew that their teacher was a college drop-out? Every time I teach I remind myself it's not about what I don't know that counts. It's about what I do know. And I'm here to teach them what I know. I'm here to teach them an application that they'll need to use in their jobs. That application doesn't care what education level you have. But you have to use it properly. And that's what I know. That's what I teach. And I do a good job of it.

IN TRANSITION
by Barbara Clayton

in transition

Growing up so fast

My role is changing. For 15 years now I have been a stay-at-home mom. My days have been filled with taking care of three very active boys, one husband, and a household. You name it, it has been in my job description. I've done it all. I've been the care giver, accountant, educator, chef, nurse, housekeeper, chauffeur, coach, advocate, laundress, entertainer, personal stylist, guidance counsellor, decorator, and event planner. I feel so blessed to have been able to stay home and I have enjoyed almost every minute of it. I have felt very fulfilled in what I do.

As the boys are growing older, and moving into adulthood, I find that my job is changing drastically. We sent Matthew off to College this year and will send Spencer off in September. While they may still chose to live at home and commute to school, I know that my role needs to adjust from one of being the mother of boys to being the mother of adults. I know that I need to step back and allow them the chance to spread their wings and ultimately soar. No longer will I be the authority figure in their life, telling them what to do and not to do. Rather, I will need to take on the role of cheer leader, cheering for them as they move ahead in their hopes and dreams and being there for them if they need advice or a shoulder to lean on.

I know that this whole transition is going to be very difficult for me and I apologize in advance to my boys for the many times where I will slip. I'm just glad that I still have time to learn and adjust to my new role since it will be another 4 years before Cameron will be pursuing his dreams in college.

STEP ① IDENTIFY YOUR WHY

Who might like to hear more about YOU and the jobs or roles that are part of your life today?

_____

_____

_____

_____

How might sharing your story benefit those people?

_____

_____

_____

_____

How might YOU benefit from exploring this topic?

_____

_____

_____

_____

If YOU don't share your story, who will?

_____

_____

_____

_____

Learn by Kelly-Ann Halbert
Supplies: That Connection by
Lauren Grier; Digital Scrapbook
Day Free Template by Crystal
Livesay. Font: FG Rebecca Script.

In Transition by Barbara Clayton
Supplies: Cardstock – Bazzill
Patterned paper – We R Memory
Keepers, Creative Imaginations,
Sandylion, My Mind's Eye; Ink
– Tim Holtz; Labels – Avery;
Thickers – American Crafts.

Stepping Back to See the Big Picture

Think for a few minutes how your work life may be different from those who came 50, 75 or 100 years before you ... or who will follow 50, 75 or 100 years from now. What kinds of things do you wish you knew about your ancestors?

What kinds of things do you think future generations will wish they knew about you? Use your answers to those questions to help guide you when deciding how to document the jobs you do at this moment in time.

STEP ② **BRAINSTORM STORY IDEAS**

My Job(s)

Explore the role your job plays in your current life by considering the following...

✏ Why do you do the job that you do? Was it by choice or necessity? What factors went into the decision?

✏ Do you have a career? Or do you have a job? Is the distinction between the two important to you?

✏ What kind of training is/was required for you to be able to do the job you do?

✏ What are your career goals? Where are you currently on the path to those goals?

✏ What arrangements have you had to make in order to do the work you do? (Consider childcare, transportation, location, etc.)

✏ What tools & technology are important to your line of work? How has this changed over time?

✏ Is the way you dress or eat affected by your occupation?

✏ How much of your day is dictated by your job?

✏ How does a typical workday compare to a day off?

✏ How would your life or that of your family be different if you did not do the job you do?

✏ What are your job-related costs? (Consider childcare, clothing, transportation, meals, etc.)

✏ What is your dream job?

✏ What do you like/dislike about your job?

✏ What role does location play in your choice of jobs?

✏ Are you defined by your job?

✏ How does this job affect your economic status? How do your wages compare to your friends, family, peers? Are you where you want to be in this area?

✏ Is your occupation one that garners respect from others?

✏ If not you, who has your dream job? What about that person's job appeals to you?

✏ How do you feel about your co-workers? Your boss?

✏ How do you anticipate life will change when you retire from working? Or do you plan to retire? Or have you already?

✏ How has your job changed since you first started or pursued this field?

✏ How does the reality of your current job compare to your expectations before you started?

✏ How do you anticipate your job will change in the next 5, 10, 15 years? How do you feel about that?

✏ Does your job feel like "work"?

✏ What do you "wish" in terms of your job?

Story List

Jot down any story ideas that come to mind as you work through the prompts.

1
2
3
4
5
6
7
8
9
10
11
12
13
14
15
16
17
18
19
20
21
22
23
24
25
26

STEP ③ GET THE WHOLE PICTURE

Photo Ideas

☐ Your work environment... close-ups of the area where you work, as well as the bigger picture, including building exteriors, signs, break areas, etc.

☐ The people with whom you come into contact on a normal day.

☐ Getting ready for work in the morning.

☐ Transitioning from home to work and/or back again.

☐ The tools used in your occupation.

☐ The different tasks you do throughout your work day.

☐ The clock at different times of the day plus the activities you do at those times.

☐ Your workplace during various parts of your daily routine.

☐ Your paycheck and/or time card.

☐ Your work attire.

☐ Appointment book or desk calendar.

☐ Your purse, briefcase or bag and its contents.

Use your answers to the following to help identify potential images or items that could help you tell today's story...

If you have access to work-related photos or memorabilia from earlier generations, gather a few items and take a closer look... what story do they tell?

_____
_____
_____
_____

What information is missing or unclear?

_____
_____
_____
_____

How might your understanding of that time period be different if you had more information through images, objects or words?

_____
_____
_____
_____

If you could go back in time, what kinds of images or items would you now gather to help tell the story of the work that was done in that time period?

_____
_____
_____
_____

The Many Little THINGS I Do

I am a stay at home MOM. My day, my life, is full of little jobs. The big picture is hard to see at times with the forest of little pictures I deal with on a day to day basis. I don't have one job. I have many. My DAY is long and full. I am a cook, providing breakfast, lunch and dinner for my FAMILY. I am a maid. I mop the floor, clean the bathtubs, wipe down the counters, change the sheets, do the laundry. I am an accountant, managing the finances, setting the budget, provisioning the household supplies. I am a TEACHER helping my KIDS with their homework, showing by example the behavior & morals that are important to our family. I am a PARTNER to my husband providing warmth & love, keeping myself healthy & informed to provide him with mental, physical & emotional companionship. I am an EMPLOYEE to 2 differnt companies, working part time answering questions for a little extra spending money of my own. I am an ARTIST creating layouts for designers in exchange for free product. I also create things in yarn and have a business on etsy. Once I had just the one JOB, analysing data for a calll center. I had regular hours, health care, paid vacation, sick leave & overtime. I traded it when my SON was born for the many little jobs I have now. No set hours, no sick leave no overtime pay. The adjustment was hard. No lie. Very hard indeed. But now, 7 years on, I can honestly say that I LOVE my little jobs.

little jobs

LITTLE JOBS
by Stacey Truman

Supplies: Fantabulous You by Eva Kipler and Julie Billingsley; Write Stuff Word Cuts by Darcy Baldwin and Misty Cato. Font: Rachel M by Darcy Baldwin.

STEP ④ BE INSPIRED

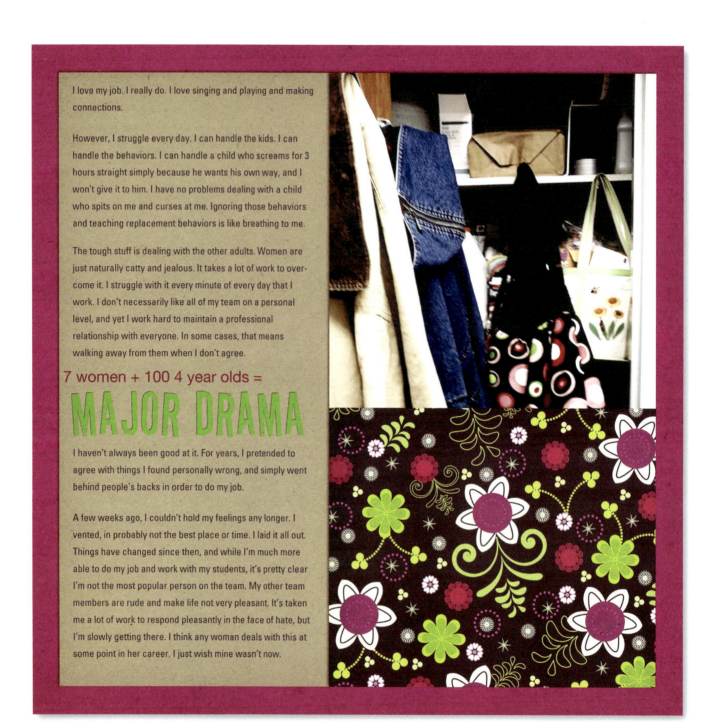

I love my job. I really do. I love singing and playing and making connections.

However, I struggle every day. I can handle the kids. I can handle the behaviors. I can handle a child who screams for 3 hours straight simply because he wants his own way, and I won't give it to him. I have no problems dealing with a child who spits on me and curses at me. Ignoring those behaviors and teaching replacement behaviors is like breathing to me.

The tough stuff is dealing with the other adults. Women are just naturally catty and jealous. It takes a lot of work to over-come it. I struggle with it every minute of every day that I work. I don't necessarily like all of my team on a personal level, and yet I work hard to maintain a professional relationship with everyone. In some cases, that means walking away from them when I don't agree.

7 women + 100 4 year olds =
MAJOR DRAMA

I haven't always been good at it. For years, I pretended to agree with things I found personally wrong, and simply went behind people's backs in order to do my job.

A few weeks ago, I couldn't hold my feelings any longer. I vented, in probably not the best place or time. I laid it all out. Things have changed since then, and while I'm much more able to do my job and work with my students, it's pretty clear I'm not the most popular person on the team. My other team members are rude and make life not very pleasant. It's taken me a lot of work to respond pleasantly in the face of hate, but I'm slowly getting there. I think any woman deals with this at some point in her career. I just wish mine wasn't now.

MAJOR DRAMA
by Kimberly Lund

Supplies: I Can Only Imagine Paper Pack by Miss Kim Designs. Fonts: Univers, 2 Peas Task List, Helvetica Neue.

PHOTOGRAPHER

by Jennifer DeLorenzo

Supplies: Classic Cardstock Authentic, Classic Cardstock Sleep Softly, Notebook Paper No. 1, Naturally Krafty No 7, Tied Fasteners No. 3, Frightful Kit, Candid Kit, Flossy Stitches – White, and Tabbed Dates by Katie Pertiet; Zig Zag Stitches by Anna Aspnes; Love Today Word Art by Art Warehouse; Have a Heart No. 2 & No. 3 and DIY Chipboard Bytes by Pattie Knox; Samara Paper Pack by Jesse Edwards; Caesilia Solids by Michelle Martin; Everyday Twill by Ali Edwards.

my Passion

[pho·to·graphs]

It is still hard for me to tell people I am a photographer. I know it is what makes me happy. I know that I have a natural eye, but I trip on the technical side and it seeks away my confidence. I absorb myself in learning all I can. But, I know my business can't grow unless I jump in with both feet and one little toe isn't cutting it. With each happy customer I become more comfortable with my skills. I just have to realize that I may never know it all. I will always be the student and that might not be such a bad thing.

CAPTURE THE MOMENT. CAPTURE THE MOMENT. **CAPTURE THE MOMENT.**

WORLD'S BEST BOSS

by Michelle Godin

Supplies: Desk Mess by Holliewood Studios; About by Creashens, Something Blue Studios and K Studio; Everyday by Lauren Reid; Mark It Up by Lauren Grier; Layered Photo Blendz No. 2 by Anna Aspnes.

I love my job!

YOU ARE HERE

This is *me.* at work

WORLD'S BEST BOSS

I never imagined I'd ever be the boss of anything. I really prefer to sit in my cubicle and do my job. Alone.

When they asked me to take over as Team Leader in March 2009 I was petrified. My first thought was: NO! I CAN'T DO THIS!

ME? A boss? With employees? And responsibilities? And pressure? Are you kidding me?

But here I am now with 11 months of Team Leading under my belt and it's remarkable how much I've changed.

I used to dread going to meetings. The thought of having to speak up in front of others made me sick to my stomach. Now I call the meetings myself and speak my mind with confidence.

I used to be afraid to share my ideas. Afraid they weren't good enough. Now I probably share more than my colleagues would like!

I used to consider myself a follower – how could I ever lead? With zero management training, this part scared me the most. But I quickly learned how to delegate. How to listen. How to teach. I am organized and efficient and I keep things running pretty smoothly, if I may say so myself!

Am I the World's Best Boss? Doubtful. But I do give it my best every single day. And nobody was more surprised than me to learn that YES, I actually CAN do this.

I am MORE than I know *myself* to BE.

to do
- schedules ✓
- research ✗
- meetings ✓
- database work ✓

22/02/10

The fact that I am teaching in the midst of huge budget cuts in a state that is ranked No. 50 in the nation makes me reflect upon why I do what I do—teach—during a time of hopelessness. I do fear that the bureaucracy has broken the system and I do not know if it can be fixed—and that is the frame within which I operate—BUT I do not teach because the bureaucracy exists or drives the direction in which education goes, I teach because I want a room with a view—I want to feel as though I am making a positive contribution to the future, and I believe I am doing so.

A room with a view allows me to see past the hopeless feeling of today...
me to see a tomorrow in which my students will find success...
me to see the reflection of the sun upon my students' faces today...
my students to see the possibilities their future holds...
me to understand the reasons behind the decisions with which I may not be in agreement...
me to hope for the future...

THE JOB

by Valerie Pfeffer

Supplies: ArtPlay Palette Mini Kit No. 06 and No. 08, and Magic FotoBlendz Layered Template Album: Parts 01 12x12 by Anna Aspnes; Hinge Pack 3, Collageables No. 02, My Family Genealogy Clippings No. 02, Classic Cardstock: My Peony and Botanist Notebook No. 02 Paper Pack by Katie Pertiet.

HOMESCHOOL

by Crystal Livesay

Supplies: Funky Old School by Rachel Young, Kate Hadfield and Pixel Works; Photo Abuse 1 by Something Blue Studios; Clumpers Circles by Crystal Livesay; Essential Stitches 5 by Syrin.

" *Don't get so busy making a living that you forget to make a life.* **"**

- Unknown source

I am torn... I am torn between being a stay-at-home mama and wanting to provide for my family financially. Before becoming a mama, I worked for 10 years in corporate America, making a very good salary, however I was extremely burnt-out. When Jake came, I went part-time for a year before we made the decision for me to leave my job and stay home full time. It was a hard transition and thinking that I'll have all this time on my hands, I decided to start a scrapbooking for others business. I took the money that I saved from a part-time job of showing houses for Realon the last 4 years and my vacation payout from my corporate job to design a website, promotional materials, and setup booths at wedding and baby shows. The response has been very good, but has not led to much in business. It is just a funnel of money going down the drain. Now, I am torn... I have realized that I do not want this business... I should have never started the business. I do not want to scrapbook other's memories when my photos are piling up around me waiting to be documented. I feel really guilty about the money I spent getting the business started and because of that guilt, I feel like I cannot quit. Truthfully, I want to be a stay-at-home mama to Jake. He is growing so fast and I want to be able to enjoy every minute of this time. In just a few short years he will be in school and then maybe it will be the right time to start this business. Or, maybe some other business or opportunity will come along. February 2010

TORN

by Rebecca Kuchenbecker

Supplies: All in a Day's Work by Libby Weifenbach and Heather Roselli; Cloud 9, Playtime, Artist Canvas and Where Flowers Grow by Kristin Cronin-Barrow; PJ Kids by Lliella Designs; Barber Shop and Do You Believe in Magic? by Libby Weifenbach; Hard Times by Penny Springman; Apple Blossom by Kristin Cronin-Barrow and Meg Mullens; Friends by Choice, Promising and Live Your Life by Traci Reed; Java Jive by Shawna Clingerman and Fee Jardine; Scrap in a Snap Set 10 by Cindy Schneider; Torn Alpha Overlay by Something Blue Studios. Font: Courier New.

WORK AND ME
MINI-ALBUM

by Jessica Bree Thompson

If you find you have several stories to tell in relation to the jobs you do, consider creating a mini-album dedicated to the topic.

> " *Do what you love and the rest will follow.* "
> — Unknown source

Supplies: Papers - Collage Press, Pink Paislee, Imaginisce, Making Memories, KI Memories; Stickers and alphas - American Crafts, KI Memories, Basic Grey, Lil' Davis, Prima; Other embellishments - KI Memories, Making Memories, Maya Road; Book/folio - 7 Gypsies; Pens - Faber Castell, Stampin' Up! Fonts: Century Gothic, Sketch Rockwell, AL Worn Machine, Charcoal CY, Marketing Script, Scrypticali, Turn Table BV.

STEP ⑤ PULL IT ALL TOGETHER

Approaches to Consider

📁 Create a map or timeline of your career path.

📁 Share your typical daily schedule.

📁 Journal your stream of consciousness during a typical work day (ie. What's really going through your head during the long meeting?)

📁 Create a diagram of yourself outfitted with the tools you need to get you through the day.

📁 Write instructions on how to do your job. This could be serious or a humorous approach.

📁 Create a then & now comparison of your occupation at different stages of your life.

📁 Depict what your role would be "worth" if you were paid for your stay-at-home job.

Materials to Use

_____

_____

_____

_____

_____

_____

Ideas to Try

_____

_____

_____

_____

_____

_____

_____

_____

THEN

When I grew up in the 70's and 80's, a phone was physically attached to the wall. Possibly, if there was a second phone in the house it was 'portable' in the sense that you could carry it into another room and plug it into a phone jack there (assuming there was a phonejack there and probably there was not) and then use it, but you were still tethered in place by a cord. Maybe, if you parents really loved you, you might have had a princess phone in your room, which had a longer cord so you could roll around on your canopy bed and hang upside down off the side while talking to your best friend about what this guy said to this girl about this other girl. The only other way to talk to someone was by sending a letter. You had to write it out by hand, spelling WHOLE WORDS and using correct PUNCTUATION. Then you put it in an envelope, addressed it, put a stamp on it and dropped it into a mailbox. The postman would deliver it 3 to 7 DAYS later. Then you had to another 3 to 7 days for a response. Then cell phones and pagers were invented and you could send a short message to a pager & that person could call you back. Cell phones were physically mounted in cars. The portables were large ugly and bulky. All they did was make phone calls, nothing else. Few people had them

CONNECTIONS

NOW

Then the cell phones got sleeker. And you could send longer messages to pagers. Home phones came in different sizes & shapes. They became portable with only the base unit tied in place. The handset could roam all over the house with you. Though this convenience does cause phones to be misplaced frequently, which was never a problem when your phone was mounted to the wall. Cell phones became able to receive text messages. The internet spread across the land and instead of sending letters, people sent email which was delivered in only minutes. You didn't have to wait days for response anymore We could instant message with people, typing in text abbreviation speak almost instantaneously, sharing photos as we did. Groups could chat by instant message. Video cameras became part of computers and Skype was created, allowing for face to face calls over the internet. Cell phones became smarter. They connected to the internet so you could instant message on them. They take photos you can sent to others by phone. You can conference call on them. They are an insidious part of everyday life now. We are always connected

CONNECTIONS

by Stacey Truman

Supplies: Over the Edge by Lauren Grier and Eva Kipler. Font: Rachel M by Darcy Baldwin.

THEME TWO

THE WAYS WE CONNECT

Goal:
Create a scrapbook page that shares the story of how you connect with other people in your life at this point in time.

While your job helps define your role in society and sheds light on your interests and priorities, the way you connect with others can really help portray your lifestyle and your personal preferences in how you relate to and feel about the world around you.

Thanks to modern technology, we have nearly unlimited options for reaching out and interacting with those around us. Unlike our ancestors who likely had to travel for days to make contact with others on the same continent, we are now able to connect with people from all over the world almost instantaneously.

Not only is it easier to cover enormous distances, we now have many options that allow us to choose the mode of communication that truly suits our own preferences. These modern conveniences have opened many doors, yet it could be argued that our new ways of connecting also lack some of the value inherent in the old ways of relating to one another, such as the face-to-face contact or a slower, more relaxed pace.

In addition to technological advances, many are also now influenced by new trends in society that affect our interpersonal connections ... reality TV shows, online dating, cyberbullying, and the ease and frequency with which we can relocate to new towns and neighborhoods, just to name a few. The number of people we connect with may be far higher than those who came before us, but the real story is how we feel about the quality and value of those connections.

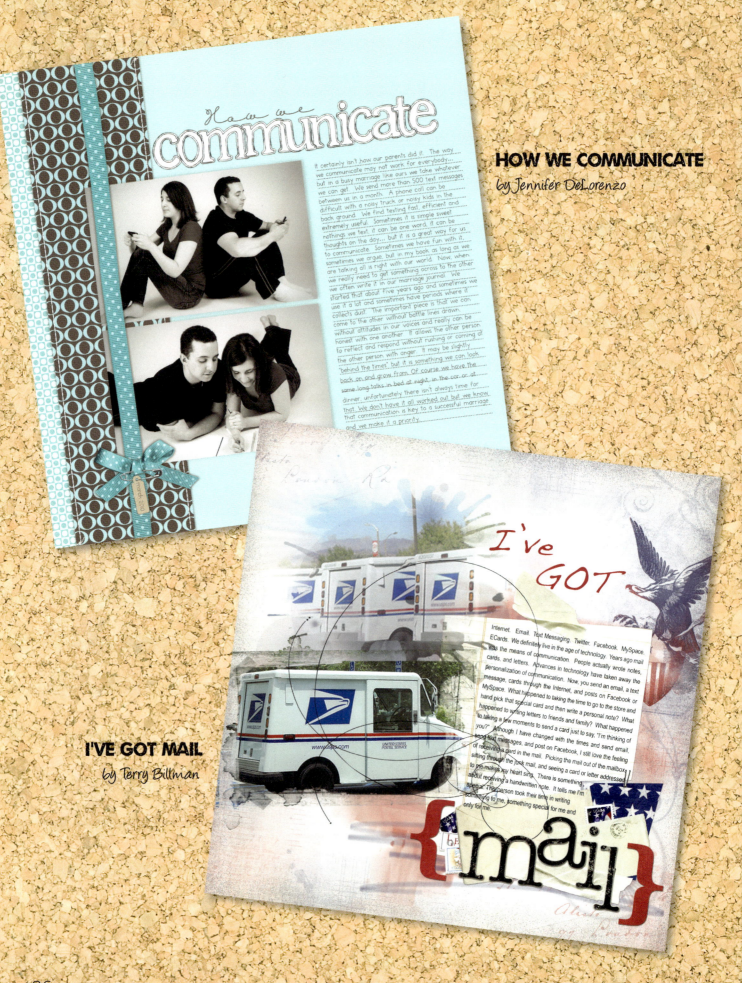

How we
communicate

It certainly isn't how our parents did it. The way we communicate may not work for everybody... but in a busy marriage like ours we take whatever we can get. We send more than 500 text messages between us in a month. A phone call can be difficult with a noisy truck or noisy kids in the back ground. We find texting fast, efficient and extremely useful. Sometimes it is simple sweet nothings we text, it can be one word, it can be thoughts on the day... but it is a great way for us to communicate. Sometimes we have fun with it, sometimes we argue, but in my book as long as we are talking all is right with our world. Now, when we really need to get something across to the other we often write it in our marriage journal. We started that about five years ago and sometimes we use it a lot and sometimes have periods where it collects dust. The important piece is that we can come to the other without battle lines drawn, without attitudes in our voices and really can be honest with one another. It allows the other person to reflect and respond without rushing or coming at the other person with anger. It may be slightly behind the times but it is something we can look back on and grow from. Of course we have the same long talks in bed at night, in the car or at dinner, unfortunately there isn't always time for that. We don't have it all worked out but we know that communication is key to a successful marriage and we make it a priority.

HOW WE COMMUNICATE
by Jennifer DeLorenzo

I'VE GOT MAIL
by Terry Billman

I've GOT

Internet. Email. Text Messaging. Twitter. Facebook. MySpace. ECards. We definitely live in the age of technology. Years ago mail was the means of communication. People actually wrote notes, cards, and letters. Advances in technology have taken away the personalization of communication. Now, you send an email, a text message, cards through the Internet, and posts on Facebook or MySpace. What happened to taking the time to go to the store and hand pick that special card and then write a personal note? What happened to writing letters to friends and family? What to taking a few moments to send a card just to say, "I'm thinking of you?" Although I have changed with the times and send email, send text messages, and post on Facebook, I still love the feeling of receiving a card in the mail. Picking the mail out of the mailbox, sitting through the junk mail, and seeing a card or letter addressed to me makes my heart sing. There is something about receiving a handwritten note. It tells me I'm special. This person took their time in writing something to me, something special for me and only for me.

{mail}

STEP ① IDENTIFY YOUR WHY

Who might like to hear more about YOU and the ways you connect with others in your life today?

_____
_____
_____
_____

How might sharing your story benefit those people?

_____
_____
_____
_____

How might YOU benefit from exploring this topic?

_____
_____
_____
_____

If YOU don't share your story, who will?

_____
_____
_____
_____

How We Communicate
by Jennifer DeLorenzo
Supplies: Neroli Paper Pack,
Miranda Paper Pack, and Dotted
Journalers by Michelle Martin;
Straight Line Stitches: White by
Anna Aspnes; Silly Billy Alpha by
Lynn Grieveson; Krafty Safety
Tags by Katie Pertiet.

I've Got Mail by Terry Billman
Supplies: Magic FotoBlendz
Layered Template Album: Part 01
12 X 12 and FotoBlendz Clipping
Masks No. 12 by Anna Aspnes;
Uncle Sam Mini Kit by Lynn
Grieveson; Botanist Notebook
No. 23 Paper Pack, 2nd Hand
Memories, Fall Orchard and
Chipboard Alphabet: Black
by Katie Pertiet; DIY Acrylic
Alphabet by Pattie Knox. Fonts:
Handwriting-Dakota, Arial Narrow.

Stepping Back to See the Big Picture

Do you remember pen pals? Getting letters in the mail? Rotary phones and party lines? Wondering if someone tried to call because you had no way to know without the advent of answering machines, call forwarding, cell phones? Think about how your methods of connecting compare to those of your parents or grandparents. Can you imagine your great-grandmother in her youth posting an ad with a dating service? Would she ever have dreamed of having a long-distance conversation in the middle of a busy highway or while attending a social gathering? Or of keeping her friends in the know through frequent status updates? Do you think, though, that she was lonely? The times have certainly changed...

STEP ② BRAINSTORM STORY IDEAS

My Connections

Explore the ways you connect with others in your current life by considering the following...

✎ How do you connect with the people with whom you interact on a regular basis? How did you first meet?

✎ Do you feel differently about people you meet online as opposed to those you know in person?

✎ How do you think your quality of life has been affected by the way you choose to connect with others?

✎ How would your life be different if you were no longer able to use your present communication tools?

✎ Do you send holiday, birthday, thank yous, condolences or other greetings by "snail" mail? Electronically? How do you feel about sending these? How do you feel about receiving them?

✎ Do you know your neighbors? What influences your relationship with the people that live in your neighborhood? How does that compare to life when you were a child?

✎ What do you like about the ways & methods you choose to connect with others? What do you see as the drawbacks?

✎ How would you describe your "social life"?

✏ What role do the connections you have with others play in your life?

✏ Have you ever had a pen pal? Do you know any children today that have one?

✏ Given a choice, what is your preferred method of connecting with others? What is your least favorite?

✏ Do you ever feel lonely? Do the connections you make relieve that feeling? Do they contribute to it?

✏ Are you a fan of reality TV shows? What are your thoughts about the way relationships are portrayed on these shows and their impact on society?

✏ Is the care you take in your interactions with others influenced by the way you connect with them? For instance, would you say the same thing to someone face-to-face as you would online or in a text message?

Story List

Jot down any story ideas that come to mind as you work through the prompts.

1
2
3
4
5
6
7
8
9
10
11
12
13
14
15
16
17
18
19
20
21
22
23
24
25
26

STEP ③ GET THE WHOLE PICTURE

Photo Ideas

☐ Images of the people you connect with, either in person or via other methods.

☐ Screenshots of messages shared online or via cell phone text messages.

☐ Tools or gadgets you use to connect with others.

☐ Images of you interacting with others, whatever form that takes.

☐ Your neighborhood.

☐ Internet, phone, cable or other connectivity bills.

☐ An empty room full of people, thanks to technology.

Use your answers to the following to help identify potential images or items that could help you tell today's story...

If you have access to communication-related photos or memorabilia from earlier generations, gather a few items and take a closer look... what story do they tell?

_____
_____
_____
_____

What information is missing or unclear?

_____
_____
_____
_____

How might your understanding of that time period be different if you had more information through images, objects or words?

_____
_____
_____
_____

If you could go back in time, what kinds of images or items would you now gather to help tell the story of the work that was done in that time period?

_____
_____
_____
_____

the {REAL} virtual me

It's a strange concept but I honestly feel that my online friends know the real me more than my 'real' friends do. I feel more comfortable writing rather than talking. In real life I tend to say nothing rather than risk saying something stupid. Online I can think before typing and then review it too. Online I can follow multiple conversations, wheras in real life I just can't do that. I can't understand anything at all if there is background noise so I am useless in a conversation with more than two people. It is difficult to make friends and be sociable when you have no idea what people are talking about and can't contribute to a conversation. For these reasons and more I value my online friendships. And although many people can't understand, these are real people sitting behind their own computers with their own reasons for wanting online relationships. Although we can't physically reach out and give each other a hug, I can still depend on them for support, laughs and friendship.

THE {REAL} VIRTUAL ME
by Eryn Herbert

Supplies: Lola Rose by Rebecca McMeen; Weeds and Wildflowers by Valorie Wibbens; Border Frames Vol. 1 by Jenna Desai. Fonts: Miama, 1942 Report.

STEP ④ BE INSPIRED

staying connected

Eleven years ago I finally caved in and purchased a computer, and Niki was trying to convince me she needed a cell phone. I actually thought Niki would be the one using the computer for the most part. Boy was I wrong! Once I learned about instant messaging and chats, I was hooked. And my daughter and I would fight over who was going to use the computer. Eleven years ago my daughter was 15 and we were the only ones in my family that had a computer. Fast forward 6 years and both my sisters had a computer in their house and I was helping my Mom choose her first computer for her home and we all had cell phones. And Niki was being deployed to Iraq for the first time.

We sent Niki off to war, putting her in God's hands, watching as the buses pulled out to take her away from us to do her duty. And then we waited to hear from her. I cannot imagine how mothers, fathers, siblings, and significant others managed in times past when their loved ones were sent off to fight across the globe in foreign places, and having to wait days, weeks, and months before receiving a letter in the mail or sitting by the phone in case they called, not wanting to miss hearing their voice. We heard from Niki within hours.

The first few months, while Niki was in training, we were able to talk to her almost daily since she could still use her cell phone. And my Mom and I even learned to text for those times when the signal was weak and that was the best way Niki could communicate with us. And we chatted online with her through instant messaging and emails. Then she left the country and we relied on the computer to 'talk' with her. There were times when she was able to make a phone call to us, and having the technology to carry our phones with us, meant we wouldn't miss that all important call. Just hearing her voice made my day.

And the computer was a way of life for us. We were able to chat almost daily, sending emails on those days when she wasn't able to get online, waiting for her in her in-box for when she could. We still relied on the post office to send her those oh so important packages from home. And with the advances in even that, she got them in about a week. We learned that even though we could communicate faster on the computer, she still loved getting real mail, something she could hold in her hand, so we still sent a few letters here and there along with the boxes, sending her a little bit of home.

But being able to chat with her and send emails and getting them from her on a daily basis made her time away in a dangerous place easier to handle. We knew almost daily that she was fine and healthy and one more day closer to coming home.

across the miles

STAYING CONNECTED
by Dawn McFarland

Supplies: Three Little Birds by Creashens; Thing Finder by Holliewood Designs; Christmas 2 by Natili Design; Wet Paint Alpha by Chelle's Creations.

ENCOURAGEMENT
by Alisa Schenck

Supplies: Everyday Ordinary by Emily Powers. Fonts: Fontastic, 1942 Report.

COMMUNI-TEXTING
by Michelle Godin

Supplies: Mindy's World by SherrieJD and Christine Honsinger; Bliss Alpha by Lauren Reid; Guy Thing by Aja Abney and Dianne Rigdon. Fonts: Pea Jacks, Matty.

Even after all this time, we still do not tell many people that we met on-line through Yahoo personals. It just has this sigma of being unsafe and unreliable. However, how does two computer professionals find love in the 21st Century? We both traveled for our careers and we weren't into the bar scene. My mom convinced me to give it a try... and within two weeks of signing up, Dave answered my profile at the end of May. He sounded like a really fun guy... almost too good to be true! LOL! We chatted for a month and then I emailed him on his birthday, June 28, and he never responded back to my email. I was hurt... however moved on. Then at the end of August, out of the blue I received an email from him asking for a date... apparently he was in Italy on business and thought he told me but never did. We made plans to go on a date September 4... and two years to the exact day, were married.

Using technology to chat is still an important part of our communication style. Daily emails are flying between us, sharing tidbits of what is going on, phone messages, and if there is anything that needs to be picked up on his way home. We are just getting into texting and do not have a text plan on our cell-phones, however we are questioning if we need to add one when we update our contracts in the fall. When I receive an email from my sweetie, makes me feel loved... he is thinking of me and needs to "talk" to me. Some may see technology as a threat to their relationship, we see it as a way to stay in contact when we can't be together.

I FOUND LOVE ONLINE
by Rebecca Kuchenbecker

Supplies: That Connection and Layered Up Scallops by Lauren Grier. Font: DJB Lauren G by Darcy Baldwin.

SEND IT OFF IN A LETTER
by Kelly-Ann Halbert

Supplies: Sending All My Love by Misty Cato; Inspired by Leslie Template Pack by Darcy Baldwin. Font: FG Rebecca Script.

It's funny how many love songs have been written that have something to do with the mail. "Write it in a letter"... "Hey Mr. Postman"... "Return to Sender". I wonder in the days to come if we'll hear of songs about falling in love over the internet, or someone breaking up by text message, or getting an email that broke your heart. All I know is that I'm grateful for the love I found online.

" Some people come into our lives and quickly go. Others stay for a while leaving footprints on our hearts, and we are forever changed. **"**

- Unknown source

FROM A DISTANCE
by Crystal Livesay

Supplies: Life Could Be a Dream Papers by Jesse Edwards; Multistitched Black/White No.1 by Anna Aspnes; Frosted Alpha No.1 Lower by Pattie Knox; ArtPlay Palette Crush by Anna Aspnes; Everyday Ordinary by Emily Powers and Paislee Press; A Beautiful Mess by TaylorMade Designs and Emily Powers; Anchors Away and Wild Thing by Emily Powers; Stitched Holes by Sausan Designs. Fonts: Traveling Typewriter, Glider Girls, SNF Daphne.

" I like to reminisce with people I don't know. "

- Steven Wright

BECAUSE OF HAYGOODS

by Kimberly Lund

Supplies: That Connection by Lauren Grier. Fonts: DJB Gimme Space, Divine, Pea Dalovely Damanda, Pea Frankie, LD Cotton Candy, Pea Heidi Jo, Pea Muggy's Girl, Pea Cuartas.

" All this technology for connection and what we really only know more about is how anonymous we are in the grand scheme of things. "

- Heather Donahue

With so much technology right at our fingertips, one would think it would be easier than ever to stay connected. i think it's just the opposite. Relationships have grown so impersonal and communication is so quick and meaningless that it's impossible to build a loving marriage using only these tools. We've made it a priority to unplug our gadgets, disconnect from the world, and take time to really connect with each other. We're so much closer because of it.

DISCONNECT FROM THE WORLD

by Jennifer Fox

Supplies: That Love Thing, That Connection and Doodle Me Stitches 4-Page Borders by Lauren Grier; Addicted to You by Madame Wing; Cloud Nine by Kristin Cronin-Barrow; Sturdy Solids by Shawna Clingerman; His Boy Elroy by Shawna Clingerman and Libby Weifenbach. Fonts: DJB Pinky Swear and How Cute Am I? by Darcy Baldwin.

WHILE PLAYING WITH PAPER

by Jessica Bree Thompson

Supplies: Cardstock – Core-dinations; Patterned paper – October Afternoon, Collage Press; Flowers & crochet ribbon – Making Memories; Paper ribbon – Jenni Bowlin; Letters – American Crafts; Bling – K & Company.

STEP ⑤ PULL IT ALL TOGETHER

Approaches to Consider

📁 Compare and contrast the different ways you connect with others and how well each of these methods works for you.

📁 Portray the various people in your life and the way(s) in which you are connected, as well as how you feel about that connection.

📁 Write a letter to your parents or grandparents describing the ways your life is different than theirs as a result of new ways of connecting to others.

📁 Write a letter to your younger self sharing advice on how to navigate the choices ahead based on what you've learned so far about the pros and cons of various ways of connecting with others.

📁 Share a conversation that is a good example of your typical communication style, whether spoken aloud, through text message, social network page, or other favorite method.

📁 Jot down your typical daily schedule as it pertains to your communication with others.

📁 Make a wish list about your connections with others. Would you like more connections? Fewer? Would you prefer a change in the quality of those connections? How do you wish things were different?

📁 Highlight the financial costs of connecting using technology in comparison to the relationship costs/benefits.

Materials to Use

_____

_____

_____

_____

_____

_____

_____

Ideas to Try

_____

_____

_____

_____

_____

_____

_____

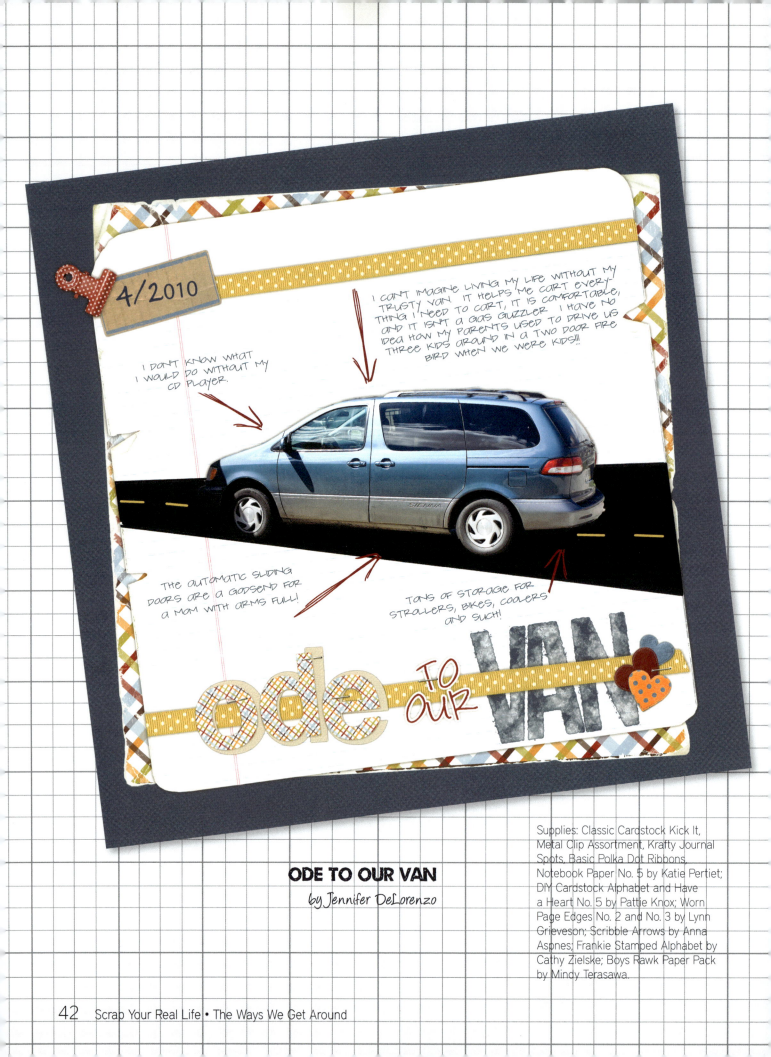

4/2010

I don't know what I would do without my CD player.

I can't imagine living my life without my trusty van. It helps me cart everything I need to cart, it is comfortable, and it isn't a gas guzzler. I have no idea how my parents used to drive us three kids around in a two door fire bird when we were kids!!!

The automatic sliding doors are a godsend for a mom with arms full!

Tons of storage for strollers, bikes, coolers and such!

ode TO OUR VAN

ODE TO OUR VAN

by Jennifer DeLorenzo

Supplies: Classic Cardstock Kick It, Metal Clip Assortment, Krafty Journal Spots, Basic Polka Dot Ribbons, Notebook Paper No. 5 by Katie Pertiet; DIY Cardstock Alphabet and Have a Heart No. 5 by Pattie Knox; Worn Page Edges No. 2 and No. 3 by Lynn Grieveson; Scribble Arrows by Anna Aspnes; Frankie Stamped Alphabet by Cathy Zielske; Boys Rawk Paper Pack by Mindy Terasawa.

THEME THREE

THE WAYS WE GET AROUND

Goal:
Create a scrapbook page that shares the story of how you travel from one place to another at this point in time.

As society changes, so does the way we travel. It's difficult to imagine a time when the only options for getting from one place to another were travel by foot, four-legged animal or makeshift raft.

The invention of the automobile vastly changed the way many of us travel, and it is no longer uncommon for a person to walk only for exercise or enjoyment. Humans have not only figured out how to fly through the air but have landed in outer space. And travel by water may now be chosen more often for recreation than out of the need to get from point A to point B.

But even with so many options at our fingertips, factors such as the environment, economy and security influence many of our transportation decisions. And with the increase in new options comes new hazards and issues, such as the choice to use a cell phone or other technological gadget while behind the wheel, drive while intoxicated, strap little ones into safety seats or buckle up ourselves.

The story of how we approach our many options available and make related decisions provides an interesting, timely glimpse into our real lives and deserves a place in our scrapbooks.

miles

mph.mph.mph.m

SOUTH
US 59

F.M.
351

JCT
181

Living in a small rural community has it's advantages. No freeways. No toll roads. No bridges. No buses. No taxis. No traffic jams. Just highways and farm to market roads. Long open roads between each small city. The roads are generally two lane roads. Rarely will you see four lane highways. Since there is no public transportation, owning a car is a must. Owning a car that gets great gas mileage is a plus since you drive long distances to get anywhere. We don't talk in terms of minutes. We speak in terms of miles. It's a given, one mile equals a minute. 70 miles takes 70 minutes.

minutes

MILES & MINUTES
by Terry Billman

GOING PLACES

GOING PLACES
by Jennifer Fox

lately we've been spending a lot of time taking bike rides as a family. we leave from our house, ride through the neighborhood, and then get on the greenway. it's a nice, safe ride and we really love it. we spend so much time in the car going from place to place that it's a wonderful change of pace to slow down and bike together. we really enjoy the time we spend together and it gives us a chance to talk and catch up with everything going on. it's a welcome break from our fast paced, always busy lives. i hope we can continue to bike together for years to come. April 2010

STEP ① IDENTIFY YOUR WHY

Who might like to hear more about YOU and the ways you get around in your life today?

_____

_____

_____

_____

How might sharing your story benefit those people?

_____

_____

_____

_____

How might YOU benefit from exploring this topic?

_____

_____

_____

_____

If YOU don't share your story, who will?

_____

_____

_____

Miles & Minutes by Terry Billman
Supplies: Absolutely Acrylic:
Arrows by Pattie Knox; Stitched
By Anna Borders White No. 01 by
Anna Aspnes; Classic Cardstock:
Pilgrim by Katie Pertiet.

Going Places by Jennifer Fox
Supplies: Life Is a Highway by
MandaBean and Eva Kipler;
Children at Play by Julie
Billingsley and MandaBean. Font:
DJB Coffee Shoppe Tall and
Skinny by Darcy Baldwin and
Shawna Clingerman.

Stepping Back to See the Big Picture

Think about how much travel has changed just in the time you or your parents have been on earth. Can you imagine what's in store for the future? As you think about the story you'd like to share, think about the questions you'd like to ask your ancestors ... the ones whose options were far more limited than your own. Where would they have gone if they'd had the opportunity? What would they have done with the time saved by more efficient travel? Or would they prefer their simpler times? Or imagine their reaction if you could go back in time and describe for them the ways we travel today. What would be most interesting to them? Most confusing? Most surprising? Let those questions guide you as you choose what to document for future generations.

STEP ② BRAINSTORM STORY IDEAS

Getting Around

Explore the ways you get around in your current life by considering the following...

✎ What is your preferred mode of everyday transportation?

✎ How much time do you spend traveling in a typical day? Week? Year?

✎ Do you drive an automobile? If so, what do you drive and why? Do you like to drive?

✎ How do you prefer to travel for recreation?

✎ How do you get to work? What factors influenced this choice?

✎ Have economic factors played a role in your transportation decisions? Is this different now than in the past?

✎ How often do you walk to get from one place to another? Ride a bike? Skate? Other non-motorized forms of transportation?

✎ Does environmental impact play a conscious role in your transportation choices?

✏ Do you like to travel?

✏ What is the most challenging aspect of long-distance travel for you at this stage in your life? What is the most enjoyable?

✏ How often do you travel outside the area where you live? What distance is considered a "long" trip?

✏ How much of your current weekly or monthly budget is designated for travel expenses?

✏ Do you take the same route to work or the grocery store every time you go?

✏ Do you have travel-related fears? What are they and what is their origin? How do you deal with them?

✏ Have national or international security issues influenced your travel decisions in the past year?

✏ What are your "bare necessities" when traveling?

✏ What do you do to pass the time or entertain yourself while traveling? Do you have favorite travel games?

Story List
Jot down any story ideas that come to mind as you work through the prompts.

1
2
3
4
5
6
7
8
9
10
11
12
13
14
15
16
17
18
19
20
21
22
23
24
25
26

STEP ③ GET THE WHOLE PICTURE

Photo Ideas

☐ Your current vehicle, exterior and interior

☐ Contents of your vehicle's glove compartment or trunk

☐ Map of your typical daily travel route

☐ View from the driver's seat on the way to a typical destination

☐ Parking tickets, toll receipts

☐ Vehicle's interior, before and after a trip

☐ Garage, shed or other location where vehicles, bicycles or other transportation items are stored

☐ Favorite travel stops

☐ Travel companions, whether a commute to work or a longer trip

☐ Gas station, including pump fuel prices

☐ Road signs, billboards, mileage markers

☐ Travel receipts

Use your answers to the following to help identify potential images or items that could help you tell today's story...

If you have access to travel-related photos or memorabilia from earlier generations, gather a few items and take a closer look... what story do they tell?

_____
_____
_____
_____

What information is missing or unclear?

_____
_____
_____
_____

How might your understanding of that time period be different if you had more information through images, objects or words?

_____
_____
_____
_____

If you could go back in time, what kinds of images or items would you now gather to help tell the story of the work that was done in that time period?

_____
_____
_____
_____

I hate flying. I'm afraid of heights and I get claustrophobic when I'm trapped in a confined space. Add to that the stress of worrying about all the things that could possibly go wrong, such as fatal crashes, acts of terrorism, or even just some bad turbulence, and it truly is a recipe for full-blown panic. In order to survive any plane ride, whether it's one hour long or ten, I need to sedate myself with copious amounts of Gravol and try my best to sleep through it.

That said, I am very grateful that humans learned how to fly. Thanks to airplanes I have visited foreign destinations that would otherwise be impossible. England, France, Rome, Cuba - all amazing cultural experiences I will never forget. What normally would be a 4 day car trip across the country to visit family translates to a quick 4-hour plane ride. Less time traveling means more time with loved ones. I also love that I can order a product online from halfway around the world and it will arrive in a matter of days via airmail. The entire world is one big shopping mall at my fingertips thanks to the mighty airplane.

Like all things in life, flying has its pros and cons, its benefits and risks. Despite my neurotic anxiety and no matter how many terrorist attacks or plane crashes are reported in the media, I would gladly take to the skies for a foreign adventure. And I'm sure glad that others are willing to do it too so that I can enjoy all the other conveniences air travel has to offer.
10/05/10

FLY AWAY
by Michelle Godin

Supplies: The Boys by Kitty Designs; Somewhere Beyond, a ScrapArtist Collaboration; Cindy's Layered Templates - Set #44 by Cindy Schneider; Kitchy Camera by Valorie Wibbens and Lauren Reid. Font: American Typewriter.

STEP ④ BE INSPIRED

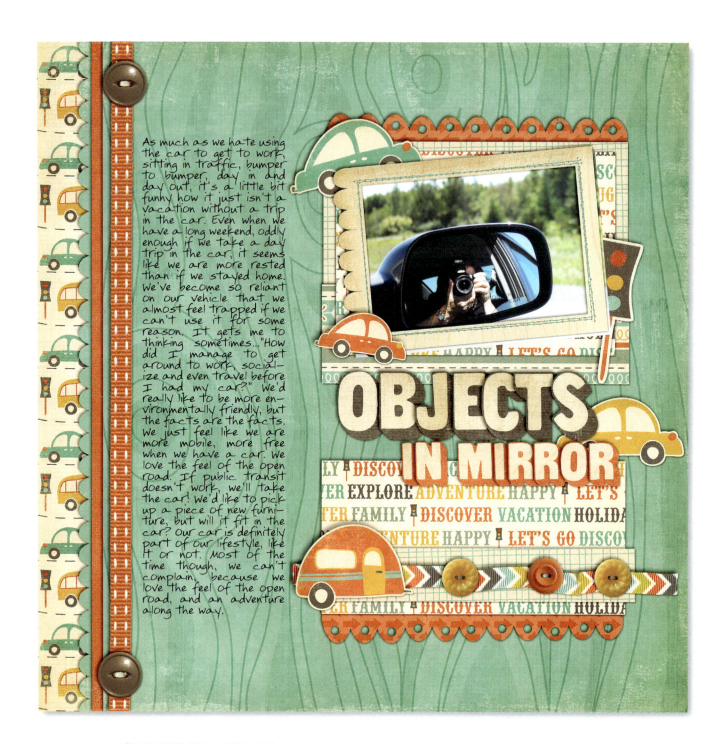

OBJECTS IN MIRROR

by Kelly-Ann Halbert

Supplies: Template by Cindy Schneider; Away We Go by Zoe Pearn.
Font: FG Rebecca.

DRIVING ANXIETY

by Crystal Livesay

Supplies: Don't Make Me Come Back There by Libby Weifenbach; Multi Stitched Black and White by Anna Aspnes; Alphabet Soup and Beauty Mark Beautiful Mess by Emily Powers; Vintage Vogue by Sahlin Studios; Kraft Addict by Valorie Wibbens; Photo Action by Kasia Designs. Font: Century Gothic.

I admit it, I am terrified of driving. There really isn't even a reason to it. Everything about it makes me nervous. What if we crash? What if the car breaks down? What if we somehow end up lost? There are too many things that can go wrong in a vehicle in my mind. So many things!! I am rational enough to know that it's the silliest thing to think about but somehow, no matter where we are going, my mind cannot control itself. We can just be out for a trip to my sisters and there will be times that we have to pull over because my nerves have gotten the best of me and I am feeling incredibly ill. I have only experience one car crash that was somewhat serious, but even then no one was hurt and it was completely out of our control, so I honestly don't know where this anxiety comes from. Most of the time I refuse to drive because I am so worried about everything. I always have to have other people driving and then I usually drive them nuts from my nerves. One day I hope to conquer this and I really hope that I do not pass it on to my kiddos. I try to keep it in check as best as I can because I really do not want them to have to live like this.

MY BUS

by Alisa Schenck

Supplies: On the Go by Katie Pertiet.

People always ask...... "What kind of vehicle do you drive having 7 children? It must be a bus!" Well yes.....kinda. It's a 15 passenger van and we call it our bus! After baby #7 we decided to upgrade from our conversion van to an extended all purpose van. It has a lot of room for the kids and all their stuff. Being one of the biggest vehicles on the road is great! I love everything about it......except the cost of putting gas into it!

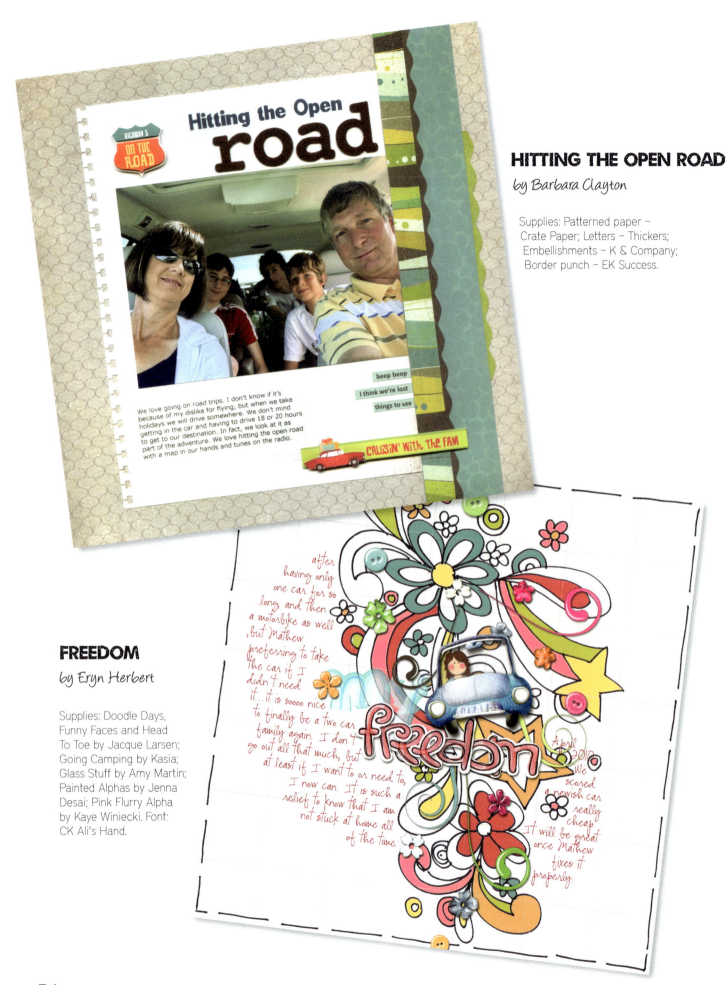

Hitting the Open road

ON THE ROAD

We love going on road trips. I don't know if it's because of my dislike for flying, but when we take holidays we will drive somewhere. We don't mind getting in the car and having to drive 18 or 20 hours to get to our destination. In fact, we look at it as part of the adventure. We love hitting the open road with a map in our hands and tunes on the radio.

beep beep

I think we're lost

things to see

CRUSIN' WITH THE FAM

HITTING THE OPEN ROAD

by Barbara Clayton

Supplies: Patterned paper –
Crate Paper; Letters – Thickers;
Embellishments – K & Company;
Border punch – EK Success.

FREEDOM

by Eryn Herbert

Supplies: Doodle Days,
Funny Faces and Head
To Toe by Jacque Larsen;
Going Camping by Kasia;
Glass Stuff by Amy Martin;
Painted Alphas by Jenna
Desai; Pink Flurry Alpha
by Kaye Winiecki. Font:
CK Ali's Hand.

after having only one car for so long, and then a motorbike as well, but Mathew preferring to take the car if I didn't need it...it is soooo nice to finally be a two car family again. I don't go out all that much, but at least if I want to or need to, I now can. It is such a relief to know that I am not stuck at home all of the time.

Freedom

April 2010
We scored a newish car really cheap. It will be great once Mathew fixes it properly.

Gone are the days of hauling around a huge stack of maps on a trip... maps, that once unfolded, were impossible to fold again. Gone are the stops at gas stations in questionable neighborhoods asking for directions from the 12 year old behind the counter. Now days we do not leave for a trip without packing a GPS system, or what we have affectionately call Vivian. She gives us turn by turn directions to get from point A to point B. Want to find the nearest Mexican restaurant? Vivian will tell us! Detour ahead? No problem, Vivian will find an alternate route in the quickest time and avoiding any tolls. I think back at my number of years of traveling for business where I would fly into a city that I've never been at 10 p.m. at night and still have a 2 hour drive ahead to find the hotel. The number of times I was lost trying to read a map and drive at the same time. How much easier... and safer... I feel today with having a GPS as my guide. I even use it in my own hometown to find rummage sales!! No more guessing as to where the road might be... think of all the time wasted! Someone is already at that sale picking up a Fischer-Price Barnyard Bingo game that I have been on a mad dash to find!! Oh, how much freedom the GPS gives us... we can be spontaneous... we don't have to plan where we are going to go before leaving the house. No more having to get on Google Maps and printing out directions. It never fails one of the map pages would fall down between the seats. Yet, there is a drawback to having this little nifty device solve all my traveling direction woes... you never know where you are!! When we had maps, we were forced to be aware of which direction is North and which side of the city you were on. Whoa be the day that we lose the GPS and have to actually read road signs!!

GONE

by Rebecca Kuchenbecker

Supplies: Passport Required and Road Trip by Creations by Rachael; Time Ticking Away by Lauren Grier. Font: Century Gothic.

STEP ⑤ **PULL IT ALL TOGETHER**

Approaches to Consider

🗁 Map out the path you travel on a normal day.

🗁 Compare & contrast your current mode of transportation with one from the past.

🗁 Create a travel diary or itinerary for a typical outing.

🗁 Interview each member of your family by asking the same question about a particular trip, such as favorite stop, travel necessities or most memorable moment.

🗁 Work the images of various travel signs into your journaling.

🗁 Create a diagram pointing out all of your favorite features in your vehicle.

🗁 List the contents of your trunk or glove compartment.

🗁 Write out a memorable or typical conversation that occurs in your vehicle ... or one that you have with yourself in your head as you drive.

🗁 Model your page after a print advertisement for your favorite automobile.

🗁 Write a fairy tale about your ideal mode of transportation.

Materials to Use

_____

_____

_____

_____

_____

_____

Ideas to Try

_____

_____

_____

_____

_____

_____

_____

_____

MEMORIES

traditions

FOOD

I grew up in a family where my mother baked and cooked everything from scratch. Very seldom did mom cook something that was boxed or prepared. As a little kid, I spent time with my mom in the kitchen playing and observing while she cooked dinner. I learned to cook at a very young age just from watching her cook our meals. I still cook most everything from scratch, using only the freshest ingredients. I am the one sibling that has preserved the old family recipes and cook the all time favorites. When the kids come home to visit, I make their favorite meals and desserts. None of the children really cook the traditional family favorites. They say their cooking, "just doesn't taste like mom's." I'm hoping with practice they will learn the recipes and pass down the tradition of making Chinese sweet bread, egg rolls, fried rice, gumbo, lumpia, pancit, watermelon rind pickles, home made cookies, and orange candy slice cake.

FOOD TRADITIONS

by Terry Billman

Supplies: A Good Life Solids Paper Pack by Jesse Edwards; Katie Pertiet Border Edge Die Cuts No. 2, Stamped Blocks No. 13 Brushes and Stamps, Party Pennant Sticks and Classic Curled Photo Frames No. 01 by Katie Pertiet; Fleurs Oranges Paper Pack by Andrea Victoria; FotoBlendz Clipping Masks No. 01, 04 & 07 and Stitched By Anna Borders White No. 01 by Anna Aspnes; Hint At It No. 03 Brushes by Lynn Grieveson; Holiday Word Art by Ali Edwards.

THEME FOUR

Goal:
Create a scrapbook page that shares the story of your relationship to food at this point in time.

THE FOODS WE EAT

The food we eat is as basic as life itself. After all, every single one of us must consume calories in order to survive. The choices we have today, however, are anything but simple.

Gone are the days where bread and milk, meat and potatoes, or beans and rice were the standard. Now it seems we are bombarded with ever-changing nutrition information, new and "improved" food products, and cultures heavily tied to the foods we eat and the ways we choose to consume them.

From fad diets to fast food, whole versus processed, school lunch programs to home-cooked meals, the food choices we make say a lot about our society and our individual lives today.

Rarely do we just eat. For most of us, our relationship to food is much more complex and brings with it a wealth of potential stories for our scrapbooks.

HEALTHY
by Valerie Pfeffer

In today's world the food we are supposed to eat is supposed to be healthy for us & to live long, happy lives we need to choose the salad and olive oil and forgo the fried food that we all seem to gravitate towards.

healthy

Nothing says LOVING like something from the OVEN

THE JOY OF

Cooking

Get Cookin' with:
Recipe For:

I've never considered myself a good cook. In fact, in the past, I never liked cooking. Then I became the mother of boys ... and more recently, teenage boys. Everything changed for me. Cooking for my boys is a real pleasure . It doesn't matter what I make because they will devour it. The first words out of their mouth when they get home from school is "Hey, Mom. What's for dinner." It doesn't matter what's on the menu, they answer "Yum!" They appear frequently while I'm making dinner just to smell it. They are willing taste testers. In their eyes, I'm the world's best cook, and I love it!

GOOD COOKS never lack FRIENDS

Oven Temperature: Time: Serves:

YUMMY delish DIVINE

THE JOY OF COOKING
by Barbara Clayton

STEP ① IDENTIFY YOUR WHY

Who might like to hear more about YOU and the ways you deal with food in your life today?

_____
_____
_____
_____

How might sharing your story benefit those people?

_____
_____
_____
_____

How might YOU benefit from exploring this topic?

_____
_____
_____
_____

If YOU don't share your story, who will?

_____
_____
_____

Healthy by Valerie Pfeffer
Supplies: Paper Lace Solids 2
by Jesse Edwards; In Distress
Blues by Lynn Grieveson; Carded
Stacked Frames No. 2, Stuffed
Edge Documents No. 1, Alpha
Scatterings, Bead Scatterings and
Messy Stamped Alpha No. 4 by
Katie Pertiet.

The Joy of Cooking
by Barbara Clayton
Supplies: Patterned paper – Basic
Grey, Fancy Pants, Kaleidoscope;
Letter stickers – K & Company;
Recipe card – Paula Deen;
Title – Cricut Base Camp;
Embellishments – Basic Grey,
Making Memories, Petaloo.

Stepping Back to See the Big Picture

Stop and really think about how different your world today is from that of your ancestors when it comes to food. Do you grow your own food? Harvest it? Cook from scratch? Spend hours canning fruits and vegetables out of necessity, rather than choice? Can you imagine a world without the option of fast food, a grocery store within quick driving distance, reliable refrigeration, electric or gas stoves and Teflon? How would your life be different if you were suddenly transported to a time 200 years earlier? Use these questions to help you choose a food-related topic of interest to future generations, who might feel today's ways are as foreign as some of the above seem to us.

STEP ② BRAINSTORM STORY IDEAS

Food & Me

Explore your relationship to food in your current life by considering the following...

✎ What governs your choice of what you and/or your family eat? Price? Availability? Nutritional value? Convenience? Something else?

✎ Where does your food come from?

✎ Does your family eat dinner together every night?

✎ Do you tend to eat the same things every day?

✎ Do you like to entertain with food?

✎ Have you ever been "on a diet"? Are you on one now?

✎ Where do you eat? Dining room? Kitchen table? In front of the TV? In your car?

✎ What feelings do you associate with food?

✎ Who does the cooking in your house? Do you like to cook? Do you consider yourself a good cook?

✎ What are your favorite foods? Least favorite? Best recipe?

✐ Are there any favorite family recipes that have been passed down for generations?

✐ How often do you eat out at a sit-down restaurant? Get take-out? Order from a drive-thru window?

✐ What role does food play in your family gatherings or celebrations?

✐ Have you experienced health-related issues as a result of your food choices?

✐ How much time do you spend dealing with food in a typical day or week - planning it, purchasing it, preparing it, eating it, cleaning up after it?

✐ What are your food-related philosophies in relation to your family? Do you cook separate meals for different family members? Utilize a school lunch program? Limit certain types of food?

Story List Jot down any story ideas that come to mind as you work through the prompts.

1
2
3
4
5
6
7
8
9
10
11
12
13
14
15
16
17
18
19
20
21
22
23
24
25
26

STEP ③ GET THE WHOLE PICTURE

Photo Ideas

☐ The foods you eat - before, during and after preparation

☐ Grocery store displays, your loaded shopping cart or basket, trunk full of bags

☐ Restaurant or fast-food establishments - building exteriors, interiors, signs, logos, order boards, menus

☐ Your daily menu or food log

☐ Tools, appliances or gadgets you use to prepare food, including close-ups of the details that tend to change over time, such as electronic panels, dials, etc.

☐ Inside your refrigerator, outside of your refrigerator

☐ Steps involved in preparing a meal

☐ Locations where you eat... table, living room, desk, car

Use your answers to the following to help identify potential images or items that could help you tell today's story...

If you have access to food-related photos or memorabilia from earlier generations, gather a few items and take a closer look... what story do they tell?

_____
_____
_____
_____

What information is missing or unclear?

_____
_____
_____
_____

How might your understanding of that time period be different if you had more information through images, objects or words?

_____
_____
_____
_____

If you could go back in time, what kinds of images or items would you now gather to help tell the story of the work that was done in that time period?

_____
_____
_____
_____

the **details**

DATE : May 2010

Drink to Good Health!

People sometimes think I am crazy that we are a soda/pop free home. My kids have never had more than a sip. I can say that I haven't had a can of pop for over 5 years. There is just no benefit to it. It is toxic waste in my opinion. I know that I can't control a lot in my children's lives but while they are in my house I can ward off the chemical creation that America calls a "refreshment". It doesn't even hydrate you! My hope is that they will someday gain an understanding and make wise choices as adults.
I'm proud to be a pop free zone.

NO THANKS

by Jennifer DeLorenzo

Supplies: Stacked Vintage Frames No. 4, Brushed Alphabet and Button Up by Katie Pertiet; Cootchie Coo Papers by Jesse Edwards; Title and Journal 12X12 Overlays, and Holiday Celebration Hand-drawn Brushes by Ali Edwards.

STEP ④ BE INSPIRED

NO COWS

by Eryn Herbert

Supplies: Spring Faieries Paper by Holliewood Studios; Fresh From the Farm by Paula Kesselring; Bordered by Emily Merritt; Paper Cut Alpha by Ju Kneipp; Symbol by Eryn Herbert. Font: Pea Ashley.

WE HEART IHOP

by Crystal Livesay

Supplies: Kitchen Counter by Holliewood Studios; Classic Cardstock Coral Charm and Color Challenge Freebie by Katie Pertiet; Stitched White No. 2 by Anna Aspnes; Around the World by Brittish Designs and Sahlin Studios; Frosted Alpha No. 1 Lower by Pattie Knox.

FRESH FOOD

by Kelly-Ann Halbert

Supplies: My Happy Garden by Kristin Cronin-Barrow; Templates Volume 4 by Nee Nee Designs. Font: All the Cool Chicks by Darcy Baldwin.

GLUTEN-FREE

by Rebecca Kuchenbecker

Supplies: Prairie Fields, Too Cute to Spook, and Art and Soul Neutrals by Julie Billingsley; Template 47 by Cindy Schneider; Colorized Photo Action by Pioneer Woman. Font: DJB Merry by Darcy Baldwin.

> " We are living in a world today where lemonade is made from artificial flavors and furniture polish is made from real lemons. "
>
> – Alfred E. Newman

" As a child, my family's menu consisted of two choices:
take it or leave it. "

- Buddy Hackett

HAMBURGLAR

by Michelle Godin

Supplies: Caught Red-Handed by Shawna Clingerman and Misty Mareda; Once Upon a Story by Emily Merritt and Designs by Lili; Kitchy Kamera by Valorie Wibbens and Lauren Reid.

STEP ⑤ PULL IT ALL TOGETHER

Approaches to Consider

🗁 Depict a typical day in your life in terms of what you eat.

🗁 Write out the conversation you have with yourself in your head as you make food choices.

🗁 Share a favorite recipe and photos of the preparation process.

🗁 Compare & contrast the food preferences of your family members.

🗁 Chart how your food choices have changed over time.

🗁 Create a layout about your favorite food - what it is, why it is your favorite, memories associated with that food.

🗁 Share something related to food that others probably don't know about you.

🗁 Create a before/after layout if you've made significant changes in your food choices at some point in your life.

🗁 Depict your food-related goals and how accomplishing them would impact your life.

🗁 Develop a "how to" page on something related to food. This could be serious, funny, sarcastic, wishful, etc.

🗁 Create a diagram of your food preparation area and label the tools, appliances and other features of interest.

Materials to Use

_____

_____

_____

_____

_____

_____

_____

Ideas to Try

_____

_____

_____

_____

_____

_____

_____

hoodies + jeans + converse = ♥

my style

If I had my way, this is what I'd wear every single day! Hoodies. Jeans. Sneakers. The uniform of casual, low-maintenance girls everywhere. I am drawn to vintage styles, (hence the Converse) and bright colours (red is my favorite) It may not be high fashion but it's an expression of who I am — laid-back and down to earth.

MY STYLE

by Michelle Godin

Supplies: Viva Friday by Christine Honsinger and SherrieJD; Luv Song Alpha by C.D. Muckosky; PotPourri Foto Frames No 2A and Double Foto Blendz Layered Template 1 by Anna Aspnes. Font: Pea Comfy Cozy.

THEME FIVE

Goal:
Create a scrapbook page that shares the story of your personal style at this point in time.

OUR PERSONAL STYLE

They say you can't judge a book by its cover, but our personal style plays a big role in how others perceive us. It reveals how we feel about ourselves, our priorities and our preferences.

Personal style includes not only our choice of hairstyle, clothing, accessories and physical appearance, but also the choices we make for our personal possessions and behaviors … the vehicle we drive, the home we live in, the way we decorate, even the way we enter a room, answer the telephone or sign a letter.

Personal style is also something that evolves over time, changing with us as we grow from children for whom most choices are made for us to adults with ideas, preferences, priorities and beliefs that have been shaped by time and life experience.

Sometimes our personal style is in perfect sync with what's inside, other times it is not. Sometimes our style is a conscious choice, other times it is merely a product of circumstance. Whatever our style, sharing an inside look at how and why it came to be adds an interesting element to our scrapbooks.

REAL DEAL
by Eryn Herbert

Flat, boring hair
tunics + long shirts
everything old and worn
Fun, short hair... maybe blue
Tight cute tops + dresses
Short skirts ; tight pants
Dark colours, boring patterns
Dark, baggy pants
Sensible shoes
my style
Colourful, bright + fun
Heels!! And no sore back.

SIMPLICITY
by Stacey Truman

Clean elegant lines Uncluttered spaces
Open areas Everything in its place No more decor than absolutely needed
One is good, more is unnecessary Simple
and stylish Let the focus point stand alone Highlight just one thing

simplicity

STEP ① IDENTIFY YOUR WHY

Who might like to hear more about YOU and the ways you express your personal style in your life today?

_____

_____

_____

_____

How might sharing your story benefit those people?

_____

_____

_____

_____

How might YOU benefit from exploring this topic?

_____

_____

_____

_____

If YOU don't share your story, who will?

_____

_____

_____

Real Deal by Eryn Herbert
Supplies: An Ordinary Day and
Doodley Doo Alpha by Valorie
Wibbens; Ruby's Room by
Kaye Winiecki; Art Dollies by
Holliewood Studios; Funky People
Parts by Crowabout Studios;
Papers and Borders by Designs by
Lili; Dreamsicle Papers by Jacque
Larsen. Font: Eight Fifteen.

Simplicity by Stacey Truman
Supplies: Simply White Papers by
Micheline Martin; Tons of Flowers
by Sara Amarie. Fonts: Brandy W
and Coffeeshoppe Venti by Darcy
Baldwin.

Stepping Back to See the Big Picture

Have you ever looked at a photo of your parents from long ago and wondered "how on earth could they have thought that was stylish?" ... and then stopped to wonder if your own kids or grandkids would think the same thing when they saw a photo of you? Take a look around your home. Check out your closet. Take a peek out in the driveway. Take a long hard look in the mirror. Will you still find the style represented there today as appealing ten years from now? Twenty? The style itself won't change. That stainless steel refrigerator isn't going to mysteriously morph into something ugly over time, but your perception of it could be much different after a few decades have passed.

STEP ② BRAINSTORM STORY IDEAS

My Style

Explore your personal style in your current life by considering the following...

✏ How much thought and deliberate choice goes into the clothing, hairstyle or jewelry you wear? How about the selection of furniture in your home or color of paint on your walls?

✏ How has your style changed over time?

✏ What has influenced those changes?

✏ What is your signature style? Is there something you always do, say, wear or carry with you that others would associate as "you."

✏ Do you like your style? What do you love about it? Hate about it?

✏ Do you tend to choose particular colors or patterns for your clothing or your home?

✏ If you don't like your style, why haven't you changed it?

✏ Can those close to you pick out your belongings or surroundings simply because they are "your style?"

✏ Which of society's style categories do you prefer … contemporary? classic? trendy? natural? vintage? something else?

✏ Do you think others perceive your style the way you'd like them to?

✏ If you had to choose a "style role model," who would it be and why?

✏ If you have children, how much of their style is really your style? At what point did/will that change?

✏ Are style trends important to you?

✏ If money was no object, would your style change?

✏ What do you think of today's popular styles?

Story List
Jot down any story ideas that come to mind as you work through the prompts.

1
2
3
4
5
6
7
8
9
10
11
12
13
14
15
16
17
18
19
20
21
22
23
24
25
26

STEP ③ GET THE WHOLE PICTURE

Photo Ideas

☐ Your appearance, both overall and close-up details, including clothing, accessories, footwear, hairstyle, etc.

☐ Your home, inside and out, particularly rooms or areas which are really "you"

☐ Specific items which reflect your "true" style

☐ Specific items which do not reflect your style

☐ Items for which you really love the style, whether you own them or not

☐ Magazine or catalog clippings showing trends or style preferences

☐ Screenshots of your Pinterest boards

Use your answers to the following to help identify potential images or items that could help you tell today's story...

If you have access to style-related photos or memorabilia from earlier generations, gather a few items and take a closer look... what story do they tell?

_____
_____
_____
_____

What information is missing or unclear?

_____
_____
_____
_____

How might your understanding of that time period be different if you had more information through images, objects or words?

_____
_____
_____
_____

If you could go back in time, what kinds of images or items would you now gather to help tell the story of the work that was done in that time period?

_____
_____
_____
_____

my STYLE

In my younger years I used to love buying all the fashion magazines. I enjoyed shopping for all the latest fashions and spent a considerable amount of my pay check on my clothes. Then ... I became the mother to three boys. Somehow, all the latest fashions didn't matter anymore. My wardrobe slowly began to switch over to jeans and tee-shirts. Even now that the boys are older the first thing I grab in the morning is a tee-shirt and a pair of jeans. I have grown into my comfortable style. These days it's all about comfort ... jeans, tee-shirt, a cozy sweater, and a pair of sneakers.

MY STYLE

by Barbara Clayton

Supplies: Paper – Basic Grey, My Mind's Eye; Letters – Heidi Grace; Embellishments – Cricut, Hero Arts.

STEP ④ BE INSPIRED

My style is eclectic, that's one thing that's for sure. I've always like bright colours and bling. I've always liked to dress up in high heels or gorgeous black leather boots. But I'm just as happy in yoga pants and a t-shirt as my birkenstock sandals will tell you. I guess maybe it's a product of growing up in the 70s and 80s but I think that's just my nature. Changeable. Flexible. oh, and it has to be comfortable, no matter how good it (or I) look.

STYLING

SOUL STYLING

by Kelly-Ann Halbert

Supplies: Lurvely by Fee Jardine, Strip Stacks by Jaclyn Bernardo.

LIFE IS DELICIOUS
by Valerie Pfeffer

Supplies: Touches of Paint, Editorial Inspiration 08012010, Curled Journal Spots No. 5 and Ad Inspiration 07252010 by Katie Pertiet; Life Is Delicious by Ali Edwards; Hint of Love by Lynn Grieveson. Font: CK Ali's Hand.

SNAPSHOTS OF MY STYLE
by Jessica Bree Thompson

Supplies: Paper - American Crafts, Dear Lizzy; Alphas - October Afternoon, Cosmo Cricket; Hearts - Fancy Pants.

SOME THINGS NEVER CHANGE

by Rebecca Kuchenbecker

Supplies: A Mother's Love by KCB and Scrap Kitchen. Font: DJB Lisa S by Darcy Baldwin.

I love Coach bags... that is no secret! Granted now that I'm not working, I do not get as many a year as I did pre-motherhood... but thumbing through a catalog or stepping into a Coach outlet store sends my heart soaring with desire. The oddest thing is that I'm so not a girly girl... so low maintenance, even more so as a mom... so what I sight I am going to the why in my yoga pants, t-shirt, and a $300 Coach bag slung over my shoulder. I had thought that the reason I desired Coach so much was to show off at work, but it's not... I am seriously in love with this leather good product and anyone who knows me, knows about my Coach collection.

I LOVE JEANS

by Jennifer DeLorenzo

Supplies: Upcycled Art No. 1 by Anna Aspnes; Photoclusters No. 16, Playful Alpha, Pick Me Up Kit and Flossy Stitches by Katie Pertiet; Chiseled Alpha No. 2 by Michelle Martin; Rag Remnants by Pattie Knox; IttyBitty Robot Kit by Mindy Terasawa. Font: Pea Emma.

I live in jeans. I dress them up. I dress them down. I think I might wear them practically every day. You would think because I wear them so much they would be easy to buy... but alas it takes me forever to find a pair that is just right. Jeans are a staple in my wardrobe. I couldn't live without them. It is funny to me the phases jeans go through. From rolling them as tight as I could, then loose with flags, back to skinny tight jeans... whatever comes next in their evolution I know for sure I will be in them regardless!!!

" Style is knowing who you are, what to say, and not giving a damn. "

- Gore Vidal

NEW LOOK

by Crystal Livesay

Supplies: Bag Queen, Young Beauty and New by Vinnie Pearce. Font: Jellyka Saint Andrew's Queen.

STEP ⑤ PULL IT ALL TOGETHER

Approaches to Consider

📁 Create a diagram with a full-body portrait of you showing your style, with labels for the essential details.

📁 Show a series of photos depicting how your style has changed over time, such as hairstyle, clothing, vehicle, home or other visible change.

📁 Create a pictorial wish list of photos or catalog items that reflect your true style.

📁 Compare and contrast your own style to that of your spouse, friend, child, parent, sibling or other relevant individual.

📁 Finish the sentence ... "I wanna be like..." and then share the reasons why.

📁 Depict today's trendy styles and share your thoughts about them.

📁 Compare the way you think others perceive you and your style to the way you want to be perceived. Better yet ... ask them and incorporate their feedback.

📁 Create a before/after page about a hairstyle change, room makeover or other significant style change.

Materials to Use

_____

_____

_____

_____

_____

_____

Ideas to Try

_____

_____

_____

_____

_____

_____

_____

stories. read.
ritten. stories. read.
es. written. stories. read.
agazines. written. stories. read.
s. magazines. written. stories. read.
books. magazines. written. stories. read.

my simple story

At least once a year I allow
myself to enjoy a fluffy
novel and to float around
the pool! This year I lost
myself in the life of
Stephanie Plum, her crazy grandma, and
the super hunk, Morelli! Who can resist the
antics of a female bounty hunter
from Trenton, New Jersey. I left my
world, my responsibilities, and my cares
behind to experience the life of one of my
favorite characters. The rest of the year,
I read essays, and pieces of "proper" literature.
This is my time and I have not found a better
way to entertain myself — on a raft with a good
book, ahhhhh!

August 2010

Bask (bâsk), v. t.   [Basked (bâskt) ;
To lie in warmth. — v. t.   To warm.

MY SIMPLE STORY

by Valerie Pfeffer

Supplies: Oh Baby Girl by Basic Grey;
Template Challenge 05092010, Classic
Embossed Grids No. 3 and Fine Line
Borders Lines No. 5 by Katie Pertiet;
Summer Word Transfers No. 2, ArtPlay
No. 10 and PotPourri Paperie Pieces
1 by Anna Aspnes; Artfully Distressed
Paper and Scraplift Chat Button by
Lynn Grieveson. Font: Pea Valerie.

THEME SIX

THE WAYS WE ENTERTAIN

Goal:

Create a scrapbook page that shares the story of how you entertain yourself and others at this point in time.

The ways we entertain ourselves and others are as varied as we are.

Some people love to entertain, others hate it. Some people seem to always be "bored" while others have lists a mile long of things they enjoy doing with their free time.

Our choices of entertainment also evolve as we grow older, though sometimes we find a favorite pastime early on that sticks with us for life.

The way we entertain ourselves says a lot about our personal preferences, our interests, our likes and dislikes, sometimes even our social or economic status. And whether we choose to entertain others and how we do that speaks volumes about our individual needs for social contact and how we fit into society in general.

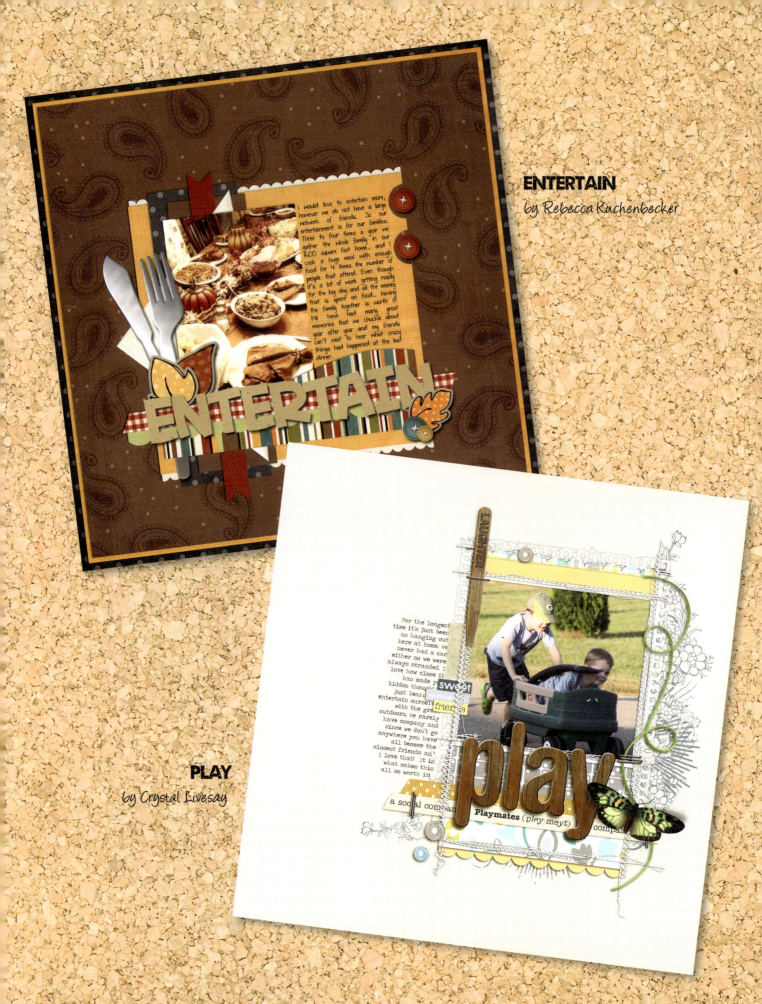

ENTERTAIN
by Rebecca Kuchenbecker

I would love to entertain more, however we do not have a large network of friends. So our entertainment is for our families. Three to four times a year we gather the whole family in our 1,600 square foot home... and I cook a huge meal with enough food for 4 times the number of people that attend. Even though it's a lot of work getting ready for the big day and all the money that is spent on food... having the family together is worth it! We have had many great memories that we chuckle about year after year and my friends can't wait to hear what crazy things had happened at the last dinner.

ENTERTAIN

PLAY
by Crystal Livesay

For the longest time it's just been us hanging out here at home. We never had a car either so we were always stranded. I love how close it has made your kiddos though, just learning to entertain ourselves with the great outdoors. We rarely have company and since we don't go anywhere you have all become the closest friends and I love that! It is what makes this all so worth it

sweet
friends
play
a social compan
Playmates (pley meyt)
compa

STEP ① IDENTIFY YOUR WHY

Who might like to hear more about YOU and the ways you entertain yourself and others in your life today?

_____
_____
_____
_____

How might sharing your story benefit those people?

_____
_____
_____
_____

How might YOU benefit from exploring this topic?

_____
_____
_____
_____

If YOU don't share your story, who will?

_____
_____
_____

Entertain by Rebecca Kuchenbecker
Supplies: Stuffed by Libby Weifenbach, Shawna Clingerman and Melissa Bennett; Template 31 by Cindy Schneider. Font: DJB Mandy by Darcy Baldwin.

Play by Crystal Livesay
Supplies: Studio Double D Layer Works No. 8 Template; SunShowers Paper Pack by Jesse Edwards; Stitched White No. 2 by Anna Aspnes; Pelican Park Solids, Yarn Swirls Summer, Nana's Buttons Chat Freebie, and Lifted Wings No. 3 by Katie Pertiet.

Stepping Back to See the Big Picture

What did you most enjoy doing on a free day as a child? Is your choice one that is still popular with youth today? How about your parents? How does your style of entertaining compare to the one you saw growing up? What would your grandparents or great-grandparents say about the ways we have fun today?

Imagine throwing a dinner party today with guests from 100 years ago. Now, can you imagine how things may change 50 years from now? What will that look like?

STEP ② BRAINSTORM STORY IDEAS

Entertainment

Explore the role entertainment plays in your current life by considering the following...

✎ What is your absolute favorite thing to do for fun when the choice is entirely up to you?

✎ Do you consider yourself to be a social person? Would you prefer to be more/less so?

✎ Is your style of entertaining - yourself or others - dictated by your current financial situation? How would it be different if money was no object?

✎ How have your entertainment preferences changed over time?

✎ How much of your daily life is spent entertaining (yourself or others) versus other commitments?

✎ What is your definition of "fun"?

✎ Are you someone who really likes to have fun?

✎ How often do you entertain others and how do you typically choose to do it?

✎ Do other people think of you as someone who likes to have fun?

✎ Where does entertainment fall on your list of daily or weekly priorities?

✎ Do you plan your entertainment?

✎ What do you think of the way society entertains itself today? For instance, do you find reality TV entertaining? Surfing the Web? Going to a fast-food restaurant? Attending a fair or carnival? Playing video games?

Story List

Jot down any story ideas that come to mind as you work through the prompts.

1
2
3
4
5
6
7
8
9
10
11
12
13
14
15
16
17
18
19
20
21
22
23
24
25
26

STEP ③ GET THE WHOLE PICTURE

Photo Ideas

☐ The scene before, during and after an event hosted by you

☐ Action scenes of the entertaining in process, either of you or those being entertained

☐ The tools, gadgets or other items that help you entertain yourself or others

☐ Something that represents "fun" for you

Use your answers to the following to help identify potential images or items that could help you tell today's story...

If you have access to entertainment-related photos or memorabilia from earlier generations, gather a few items and take a closer look... what story do they tell?

_____

_____

_____

_____

What information is missing or unclear?

_____

_____

_____

_____

How might your understanding of that time period be different if you had more information through images, objects or words?

_____

_____

_____

_____

If you could go back in time, what kinds of images or items would you now gather to help tell the story of the work that was done in that time period?

_____

_____

_____

_____

playing Scattegories, Christmas Day 2009

GAME ON!

When I sat at the kitchen table as a child and entertained myself with games, I never imagined I'd be using those exact same games to entertain guests as an adult! When I was little, some of my favourites were The Game of Life, Checkers, Clue, Monopoly, Yahtzee, and card games such as Rummy and Crazy Eights. Now my favourite party games are Scattegories or Taboo. In recent years we've made it a family tradition to play games when we get together at Christmas or Thanksgiving. I love it! So much more fun and engaging than sitting in front of the television. Humans have been playing board games since pretty much the dawn of civilization and I'm sure we'll continue to do so, no matter how technologically advanced our society becomes. There's nothing that can compare with the social interaction that comes from sitting around a table with friends and family.

GAME ON!
by Michelle Godin

Supplies: That's How I Roll by Karah Fredricks; Let's Play by Kaye Winiecki and Kate Hadfield; Desk Mess by Holliewood Studios. Font: American Typewriter.

STEP ④ BE INSPIRED

swim

Over the last year, swimming has become a big part of our lives. Last year it was about getting out of the house and getting the kids used to water. None of them could swim and we had to get my girls over their fear. So every weekend we went to the pools or the beach and they all become really confident in the water. After summer I put the 3 oldest into swimming lessons. And over the past 6 months, the change in all of them is unbelievable. All 3 of them is completely comfortable in the water. They can all swim freestyle to varying degrees and they never want to get out of the water. We still go to the pools nearly every week as a family and it has been wonderful to see them all progressing. Now that it is summer again we are looking forward to much more beach time. Even Keilan is confident in the water now...too confident sometimes. But at nearly 3yrs we don't need to be constantly holding him at the beach or pool. As long as he is in the shallows and we are close, we know he is okay. Our swimming time really has become our family time. There are no computers, tvs, work, toys, arguments or whinging. There is only the six of us, enjoying spending time together and I cherish it.

Swimming lessons are at The Swim School Beaumaris. While Steven has his lesson on a Tuesday morning, that is Keilan's special time to walk into the shops and go on the Wiggle Car. Our usual family swimming haunt is The Arena Joondalup. Lately we've also been going to Beatty Park for the slides and kids area. When we go to the beach it is usually Hilary's. Being within the harbour, it is very calm and safe for the kids. The kids also love the playground. For something different we love to go to the Lagoon. The small reef makes for relatively calm swimming for the kids, and Mathew and I can take turns to snorkel the reef. For Christmas the older kids are getting snorkelling sets so it will be fun to teach them to snorkel this year.

14/12/10

SWIM
by Eryn Herbert

Supplies: The Yellow Submarine by Faith True; Kitschy Christmas Paper by Jacque Larsen; Messy Machine Stitches – Borders by Emily Merritt; Circle Werx by CD Muckosky; Those Box Thingies by Karah Fredericks. Fonts: Jellyka Gare De Chambord, Pea Felicia.

TOGETHER

by Jennifer DeLorenzo

Supplies: DYL Template No. 1 by Cathy Zielske; Brilliantly Paper Pack by Jesse Edwards; Crumpled Neutrals and Stitched by Anna White No. 1 by Anna Aspnes; Outlined by Ali Edwards; Hinge Pack by Katie Pertiet.

WHATCHA READIN'?

by Kelly-Ann Halbert

Supplies: Bookworm by Kristin Cronin-Barrow; Template by Jaclyn Bernardo. Font: All the Cool Chicks by Darcy Baldwin.

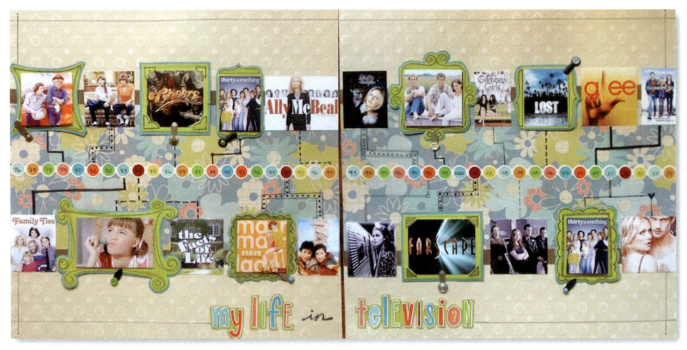

MY LIFE IN TELEVISION

by Jessica Bree Thompson

Supplies: Cardstock - Core'dinations; Patterned paper – Sassafras, Prima Marketing, My Mind's Eye; Alphas and border stickers - Echo Park.

" We aren't in an information age. We are in an entertainment age. "
- Anthony Robbins

REMEMBER:
i remember when i was first allowed to stay up past 9pm & watched cheers w/ mom. i already knew the theme song - mom asked how! i explained... i fell asleep to that song every thurs. ☺

" *If you obey all the rules, you miss all the fun.* "

- Katherine Hepburn

The first signs of spring (and bare ground) were a good excuse to pick up a kite at Captain Bob's. The girls had fun ... but Daddy's attention span lasted much longer!!

SPRING is in the air

MARCH 20, 2011

SPRING IS IN THE AIR

by Kristin Rutten

Supplies: Tortuga Template #99 by Kellie Mize Designs; Spread Your Wings by Sir Scrapalot Designs; Smile. Laugh. Play. by Studio Flergs. Fonts: Quilline Script, Traveling Typewriter.

STEP ⑤ PULL IT ALL TOGETHER

Approaches to Consider

🗁 Share a behind-the-scenes look at a party or event planned by you.

🗁 Create a daily schedule or chart that depicts how much of your day is focused on fun and how much is on other parts of your life.

🗁 Define "fun" through words, journaling and/or photos.

🗁 Compare/contrast activities you consider fun to those which are not, perhaps in a humorous way.

🗁 Journal through another person's viewpoint about an event you both attended or which you hosted.

🗁 Finish this sentence ... "The most fun I ever had was ..."

🗁 Create a "How to Have Fun" layout depicting your own personal preferences.

🗁 Interview your family members regarding their favorite ways to have fun.

🗁 Develop a timeline showing how your entertainment preferences have changed over your lifetime.

Materials to Use

_____

_____

_____

_____

_____

_____

Ideas to Try

_____

_____

_____

_____

_____

_____

I'm not a big shopper. I don't like going out and shopping for clothes and shoes. It's just not something that I enjoy doing. However, I love going over the border and doing some shopping in the United States. There are certain stores that I could spend hours in. Hobby Lobby, Pottery Barn, and Target are some of my favourites. For some reason, shopping in the United States is just not the same as shopping at home. It's more exciting and I look forward to it.

CROSS BORDER SHOPPING

by Barbara Clayton

Supplies: Patterned paper – Basic Grey, My Mind's Eye; Letters – Sandylion, K & Company; Embellishments – Me & My Big Ideas, K & Company.

THEME SEVEN

THE WAYS WE SHOP & DO BUSINESS

Goal:

Create a scrapbook page that shares the story of how you shop and do business at this point in time.

Few things have changed more in recent years than the options available to us in terms of shopping and doing business, thanks in large part to the explosion of the Internet.

No longer does it cost a fortune to start a business. No longer is a customer base limited by geography. For many of us, tools like credit and debit cards or Paypal seem like basic necessities rather than conveniences. Ebay is something our grandparents probably never dreamed of and Amazon.com has created entirely new definitions of customer service.

Business itself has changed significantly over time, particularly for smaller towns that may be struggling to simply survive as the result of competition from big "box stores" and the ease of traveling elsewhere to meet our needs.

Where you shop, how you shop, with whom you decide to do business... even whether you choose to be in business for yourself ... all reveal things about you that deserve a place in your scrapbooks.

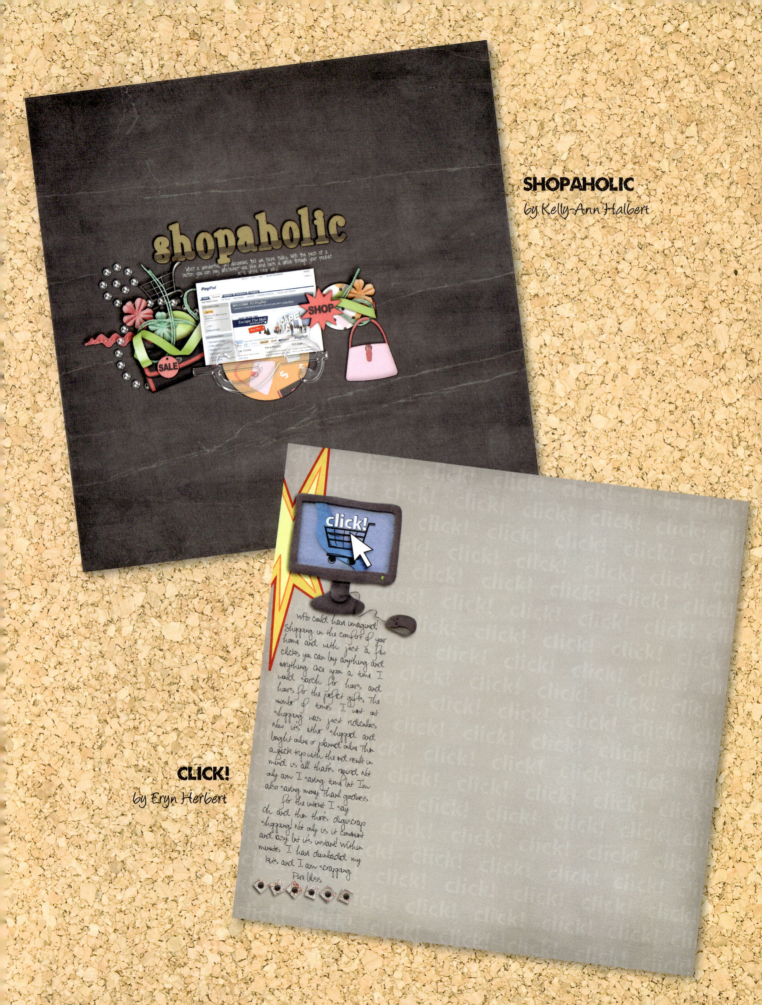

SHOPAHOLIC
by Kelly-Ann Halbert

CLICK!
by Eryn Herbert

STEP ① IDENTIFY YOUR WHY

Who might like to hear more about YOU and the ways you shop and do business in your life today?

_____

_____

_____

_____

How might sharing your story benefit those people?

_____

_____

_____

_____

How might YOU benefit from exploring this topic?

_____

_____

_____

_____

If YOU don't share your story, who will?

_____

_____

_____

Stepping Back to See the Big Picture

Do you remember how much things cost when you were a kid? If you dreamed of someday owning a business ... and now do ... does your business look and act anything like you originally imagined? Think about how much things have changed in just the past 15 or 20 years... can you predict and imagine how they will be different 20 years down the road? Do you think we'll still have the penny? Will they just scan our fingerprint to make payment? What stories do you imagine yourself telling your grandchildren or great-grandchildren about shopping and doing business in this era?

STEP ② BRAINSTORM STORY IDEAS

Shopping
& Business

Explore how you shop and do business in your current life by considering the following...

✏ When you shop, are you more concerned with quality or price? Are you a bargain hunter? Do you use a grocery list? Clip coupons?

✏ What factors influence your purchasing decisions?

✏ Where are your favorite places to shop? Why?

✏ Is supporting your local business community important to you?

✏ How often do you go shopping for fun? For necessities?

✏ How do you pay for purchases? Cash? Credit card? Debit card? Paypal? Line of credit?

✎ Do you live beyond your means?

✎ How do you feel about thrift stores? Second-hand? Antiques?

✎ What is your average monthly budget? How much is spent on food? Clothing? Utilities? Entertainment?

✎ Are you comfortable doing business online?

✎ Do you enjoy shopping?

✎ Do you own your own business … or want to?

Story List
Jot down any story ideas that come to mind as you work through the prompts.

1
2
3
4
5
6
7
8
9
10
11
12
13
14
15
16
17
18
19
20
21
22
23
24
25
26

STEP ③ GET THE WHOLE PICTURE

Photo Ideas

☐ Screenshots of favorite Websites

☐ Your chosen tools of the trade (credit/debit cards, cash, checks, etc)

☐ Piggy bank

☐ Shopping lists

☐ Ads, coupons or other marketing materials used in your shopping/planning

☐ Shots from an actual shopping trip, including exterior and interior of stores, shopping cart, cash registers, displays, signage or marketing displays, etc.

☐ Car loaded after a shopping trip

Use your answers to the following to help identify potential images or items that could help you tell today's story...

If you have access to business-related photos or memorabilia from earlier generations, gather a few items and take a closer look... what story do they tell?

_____
_____
_____
_____

What information is missing or unclear?

_____
_____
_____
_____

How might your understanding of that time period be different if you had more information through images, objects or words?

_____
_____
_____
_____

If you could go back in time, what kinds of images or items would you now gather to help tell the story of the work that was done in that time period?

_____
_____
_____
_____

CHORE

by Rebecca Kuchenbecker

Supplies: What's For Dinner by Lauren Grier and Julie Billingsley; Template 78 by Cindy Schneider.

STEP ④ BE INSPIRED

{ARMCHAIR} SHOPPER
by Michelle Godin

Supplies: Vintage Vogue Papers by Sahlin Studio; Scrapping 9 to 5 by Kate Hadfield; Junk Yard by SherrieJD; Over the Edge by Eva Kipler and Lauren Grier; Cornered 1 by Creashens. Font: American Typewriter.

SAVING FOR...
by Crystal Livesay

Supplies: Saving the Pennie's Doodles by Kate Hadfield; Papparazzi Cardstocks by Polka Dot Pixels; Baby Pink Stitches by Anna Aspnes.

THE LIST
by Valerie Pfeffer

Supplies: Stamped n Framed LT No. 13, Halloween Memories Cardstock 01, Sealife Memories Alpha, Watery Washes, Rimmed Journalers No. 1 – Black, Sampler 10, and Home and Garden File Tabs 3 by Katie Pertiet; Stitched by Anna Threads White by Anna Aspnes; Metal Hearts by Jesse Edwards. Font: 1942 Report.

> " *The quickest way to know a woman is to go shopping with her.* "
> — Marcelene Cox

TECH-SAVVY

by Jessica Bree Thompson

Supplies: Cardstock - Core'dinations; Papers - Echo Park, Sassafras, We R Memory Keepers; Ink/mist - Tattered Angels; Border sticker - We R Memory Keepers; Alphas - Heidi Swapp, Making Memories; Stickers - October Afternoon.

> " *The odds of going to the store for a loaf of bread and coming out with only a loaf of bread are three billion to one.* "
> — Erma Bombeck

The UPS man knows our house all too well. If I have a choice of online shopping or going to a store you can bet that I will be searching through Amazon. If there is free shipping, in my mind there is no better way to shop. Not to mention I don't have to go from place to place to search. Everything is just a click away. Much too easy for this computer addict!! It is a beautiful thing!

ONLINE SHOPPING

by Jennifer DeLorenzo

Supplies: Page Protectors and Class Cardstock: All My Chicks by Katie Pertiet; Fasten Its No. 3, Felt Board Friends – Do It Digi and Tie Its! by Pattie Knox; Chiseled Alpha No. 1 by Maplebrook Studios.

STEP ⑤ PULL IT ALL TOGETHER

Approaches to Consider

📁 Create a list of recent or common purchases to show what the things you buy cost at this point in time.

📁 Document a typical shopping trip, including who you went with, where you went, what you bought, etc.

📁 Create a catalog-style page of items you frequently purchase or would like to purchase, including prices, where you would buy them, shipping or delivery costs, etc.

📁 Spread out the contents of your shopping bag and identify each item purchased through a diagram-style layout.

📁 Compare shopping for a specific item, such as school clothes or groceries, to your memories of another time.

📁 Create a page about your favorite purchase in the past six months, including how you went about getting it. Did you plan ahead and save for it? Comparison shop? Buy on impulse? Use credit?

📁 List all of the online shops you frequent in a typical day, week or month.

📁 If you are in business for yourself, create a page describing that business, perhaps in the form of an ad or by displaying your actual marketing materials and messages.

📁 Compare your approach to shopping with that of your spouse, child, parents, best friend or other person in your life.

Materials to Use

_____

_____

_____

_____

_____

_____

Ideas to Try

_____

_____

_____

_____

_____

_____

_____

PLAN FOR THE FUTURE

It is hard being married to an entrepreneur when you yourself isn't one. Dave has always yearned for more in life than what an engineer salary will bring him... and in the last 10 years or so, he as been trying to build a side business while working 50 hours weeks and a part time in radio. I can't be totally upset with the multilevel he has been involved in... he has met some wonderful people and has grown in his faith with God and also developed a positive outlook on life. Sadly, he wasn't able to get very far in this company and it was a bit frustrated. In spring, a friend that he met through the business came to him and they talked about forming their own company. So in May, Trim Advantage LLC was born. In June, Steve heard of an awesome company that had a great product line and compensation plan and they decided to join ranks. I'm just struggling with this new business... as I did with the previous one... I feel so sad when Dave pounds the pavement only to hear no after no. I try to keep faith in my husband, it has been a challenge to keep positive for him and not to dwell on the amount of money that is being spent during start up.

married to an entrepreneur

FINANCIAL RESPONSIBILITY

MARRIED TO AN ENTREPRENEUR

by Rebecca Kuchenbecker

Supplies: Hard Times by Penny Springmann; Dollar and Sense by Heather Roselli; Template by Lynette Nettio; SD Alpha by Studio Flergs; Mighty Small Alpha by Zoe Pearn.

THEME EIGHT

THE WAYS WE ARE CHALLENGED

Goal:
Create a scrapbook page that shares the story of the challenges you face at this point in time.

There isn't a person alive that doesn't face challenges on a daily basis.

A challenge can be as small as choosing what to eat for breakfast every morning … or as overwhelming as making a decision that will impact the rest of our lives in a profound way. A challenge can be something we seek or choose to view as an opportunity. A challenge can just as easily be that which we make great efforts to avoid and perceive as entirely negative.

Big or small, chosen or thrust upon us, the challenges in our lives and how we view and respond to them are very often one of the most defining parts of our character. As such, those challenges provide a wealth of information just waiting to be revealed in our scrapbooks.

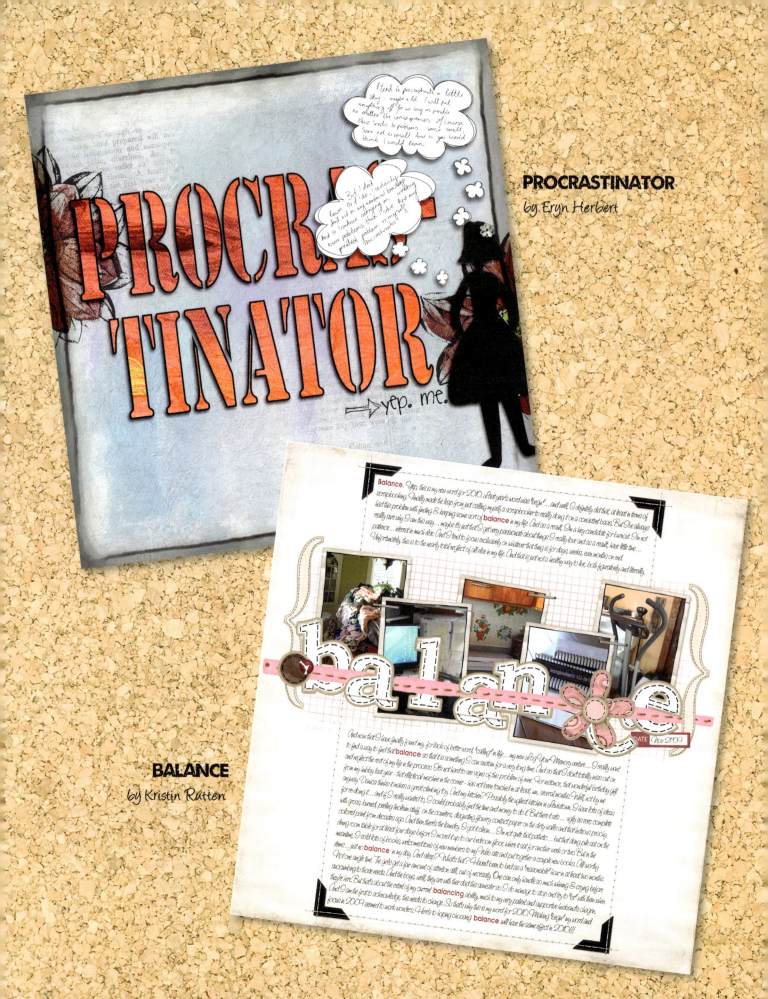

PROCRASTINATOR

by Eryn Herbert

BALANCE

by Kristin Rutten

STEP ① IDENTIFY YOUR WHY

Who might like to hear more about YOU and the ways you are challenged in your life today?

_____
_____
_____
_____

How might sharing your story benefit those people?

_____
_____
_____
_____

How might YOU benefit from exploring this topic?

_____
_____
_____
_____

If YOU don't share your story, who will?

_____
_____
_____

Procrastinator by Eryn Herbert Supplies: Vincent's Room, All About Me and Love Note by ViVa Artistry; So Chic by Jacque Larsen; What Were You Thinking by Amy Sumrall; Stitching Love by Valorie Wibbens. Fonts: Pea Courtney, Stencil Std.

Balance by Kristin Rutten Supplies: Foxy Roxy by Fee Jardine; Lil Bit Tags by Katie Pertiet. Fonts: ITC Avant Garde, Saginaw.

Stepping Back to See the Big Picture

Perhaps one of the most obvious comparisons when discussing challenges throughout history is to take a look at life today versus that during the Great Depression. Think about the last time you felt particularly challenged by a part of your life. Can you imagine your forefathers feeling challenged by that same circumstance? Are there things you feel challenged by today that earlier generations would see as a luxury? Consider your average day ... the things you do, the places you go, the expectations you feel you must meet. How does that compare to 10, 20, 30 years ago? How do you anticipate this may be different 20 or 30 years from now?

STEP ② BRAINSTORM STORY IDEAS

Challenges

Explore how you face challenges in your current life by considering the following...

✎ Are you a challenge-seeker? Or do you tend to avoid things that don't come easily to you?

✎ How do you typically approach a challenge? Are you a planner? A researcher? Do you ask friends for help? Try to tackle it on your own? Avoid it as long as possible?

✎ What has been your greatest challenge to date? How did you approach it? What was the outcome? How did you feel about it after it was over?

✎ Do you seek out others who have a similar tolerance for challenge as yourself? How do you compare to your other family members in this area?

✏ Are there challenges you would like to tackle in the future?

✏ What have you learned from the challenges you've faced so far in life?

✏ How do you respond to challenges that enter your life without your consent or control? What are some of those challenges you have faced or are facing?

✏ Are there challenges you feel are insurmountable?

✏ How would you define "challenge"?

✏ What role do you believe attitude plays in dealing with life's challenges?

Story List
Jot down any story ideas that come to mind as you work through the prompts.

1

2

3

4

5

6

7

8

9

10

11

12

13

14

15

16

17

18

19

20

21

22

23

24

25

26

STEP ③ GET THE WHOLE PICTURE

Photo Ideas

☐ Tools, books or other resources you use to tackle a particular challenge

☐ Objects that represent a challenge for you

☐ Newspaper clippings or headlines about national challenges that concern you

☐ Before/after photos of the process of tackling a challenge

☐ An image, scenario or vision of how you see or would like to see life after a particular challenge

Use your answers to the following to help identify potential images or items that could help you tell today's story...

If you have access to challenge-related photos or memorabilia from earlier generations, gather a few items and take a closer look... what story do they tell?

_____
_____
_____
_____

What information is missing or unclear?

_____
_____
_____
_____

How might your understanding of that time period be different if you had more information through images, objects or words?

_____
_____
_____
_____

If you could go back in time, what kinds of images or items would you now gather to help tell the story of the work that was done in that time period?

_____
_____
_____
_____

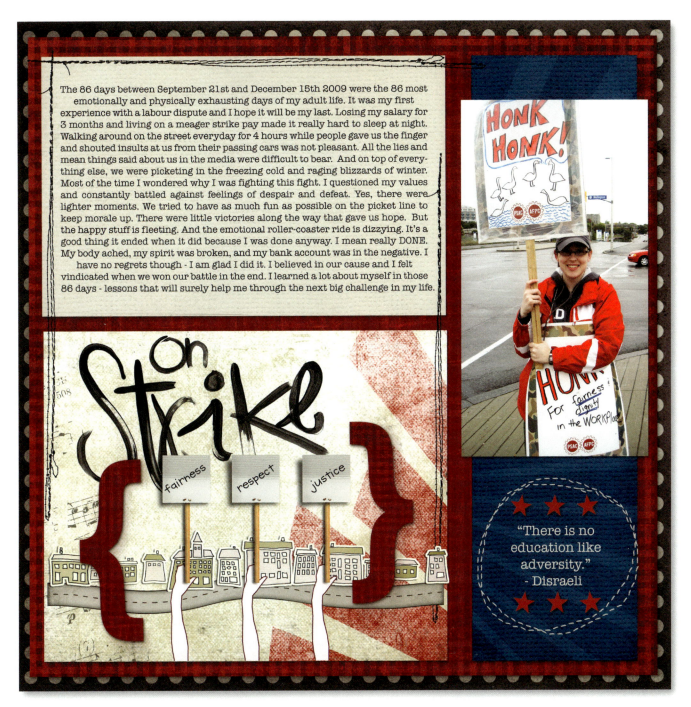

The 86 days between September 21st and December 15th 2009 were the 86 most emotionally and physically exhausting days of my adult life. It was my first experience with a labour dispute and I hope it will be my last. Losing my salary for 3 months and living on a meager strike pay made it really hard to sleep at night. Walking around on the street everyday for 4 hours while people gave us the finger and shouted insults at us from their passing cars was not pleasant. All the lies and mean things said about us in the media were difficult to bear. And on top of everything else, we were picketing in the freezing cold and raging blizzards of winter. Most of the time I wondered why I was fighting this fight. I questioned my values and constantly battled against feelings of despair and defeat. Yes, there were lighter moments. We tried to have as much fun as possible on the picket line to keep morale up. There were little victories along the way that gave us hope. But the happy stuff is fleeting. And the emotional roller-coaster ride is dizzying. It's a good thing it ended when it did because I was done anyway. I mean really DONE. My body ached, my spirit was broken, and my bank account was in the negative. I have no regrets though - I am glad I did it. I believed in our cause and I felt vindicated when we won our battle in the end. I learned a lot about myself in those 86 days - lessons that will surely help me through the next big challenge in my life.

HONK HONK!

HONK For fairness dignity in the WORKPLACE

fairness   respect   justice

"There is no education like adversity."
- Disraeli

ON STRIKE
by Michelle Godin

Supplies: Babycakes by HGD by Laurie Ann and Danielle Donaldson; Suzy Q Alpha by C.D. Muckosky; Whimsical Garden by Holly Designs; Heart and Soul by Holly Designs and Sahlin Studio; Urban Madness by Ida Designs; Jammin' by Kaye Winiecki. Font: American Typewriter.

STEP ④   BE INSPIRED

PASSION

by Kelly-Ann Halbert

Supplies: Beautimous Spring Alpha by Shawna Clingerman; Life's Rich Tapestry by Litabells Designs. Font: FG Rebecca Script.

blessings & challenges.

November 7, 2010

Parenthood is a challenge that I face daily. It is so tough to be sure you are making the right decisions every day. Are you scaring your children for life? Are you preparing them for the future? Have you given them the audience they need to keep faith and trust in GOD? Those are the big ones. But I also struggle with keeping them on top of school, eating right, grooming themselves, learning to care for their stuff and having a little fun while balancing it all. I often wonder if I hug them enough or tell them the good stuff as I am constantly telling them what not to do. It all weighs heavily on my heart as I try to get it all done. It always seems to be something and so em thing always gets in the way of what I am trying to accomplish. Ultimately I just want them to know that I love them and that they have a soft place to land if they fall. There are days when that is a difficult one to manage as I put them in time out for fighting or whining. Parenthood is a challenge and often a battle but it is an amazing blessing in my life and I love being their mom!

parenthood is a challenge

PARENTHOOD IS A CHALLENGE
by Jennifer DeLorenzo

Supplies: Layered Memories No. 127 by Michelle Martin; Up Up Away Paper Pack by Jesse Edwards; Creased Cardstock No. 3 by Katie Pertiet; 12x12 Life Text Frames and Graduation Hand-Drawn Words by Ali Edwards; In A Word Epoxies by Pattie Knox.

" Life's challenges are not supposed to paralyze you, they're supposed to help you discover who you are. "

- Bernice Johnson Reagon

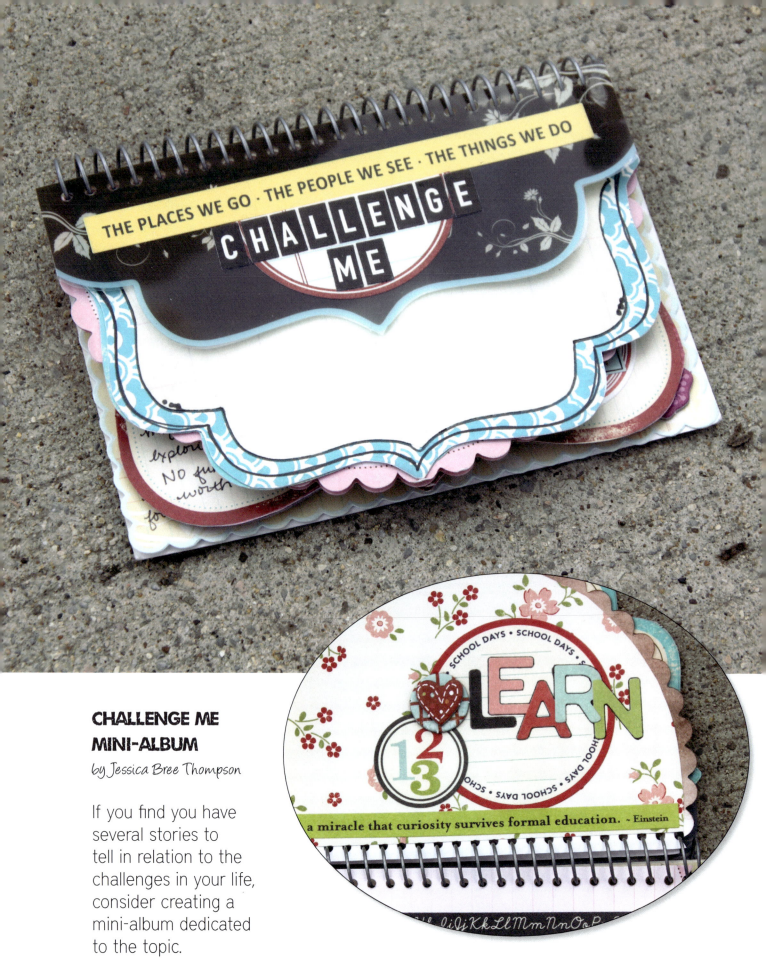

THE PLACES WE GO · THE PEOPLE WE SEE · THE THINGS WE DO

CHALLENGE ME

SCHOOL DAYS · SCHOOL DAYS ·

LEARN

a miracle that curiosity survives formal education. ~ Einstein

CHALLENGE ME MINI-ALBUM

by Jessica Bree Thompson

If you find you have several stories to tell in relation to the challenges in your life, consider creating a mini-album dedicated to the topic.

Supplies: Book - Making Memories; Patterned paper: October Afternoon, Making Memories, Basic Grey; Alphas - October Afternoon; Word and phrase stickers: October Afternoon; Journaling spots and stickers - October Afternoon, K & Company; Chipboard embellishments - Crate Paper; Puffy circles and flowers - Making Memories.

STEP ⑤ PULL IT ALL TOGETHER

Approaches to Consider

🗁 Plot the most significant challenges you've faced in your life so far along a timeline.

🗁 List the challenges you would like to tackle in the future, perhaps with a description of what you hope to gain by succeeding in your efforts.

🗁 Write a letter to an object, person or circumstance you have found particularly challenging.

🗁 Script a fairy tale or describe how your life would be different if a particular challenge was not present.

🗁 List the steps you have taken or need to take when confronting a challenge in your life.

🗁 Write instructions for someone else facing a challenge similar to one you have dealt with.

🗁 Create a before/after page about how life changes throughout the process of tackling a challenge.

🗁 Write the word "challenges" in the center of your page and create a web, map or collection of images around the perimeter depicting all of the challenges in your life.

🗁 Compare & contrast the challenges in your life versus another person, perhaps someone from an earlier generation, another family member, or even yourself at another point in time.

Materials to Use

_____

_____

_____

_____

_____

_____

Ideas to Try

_____

_____

_____

_____

_____

_____

ENJOY THIS BOOK?
Interested in spreading the word?

Please consider sharing your thoughts through a short review on our Amazon.com sales page!

It only takes a few minutes and will help keep the creative energy flowing … simply search for "Scrap Your Real Life" at **http://amazon.com** to get started.

Thank you for your support!

CONTRIBUTOR INDEX

Billman, Terry   26, 44, 58, 83

Clayton, Barbara   8, 54, 60, 106

DeLorenzo, Jennifer   17, 26, 42, 67, 86, 101, 119, 133

Fox, Jennifer   6, 39, 44

Godin, Michelle   17, 35, 51, 71, 74, 99, 116, 131

Halbert, Kelly-Ann   8, 36, 52, 69, 84, 101, 108, 132

Herbert, Eryn   33, 54, 68, 76, 100, 108, 124

Kuchenbecker, Rebecca   19, 36, 55, 70, 86, 92, 115, 122

McFarland, Dawn   34

Livesay, Crystal   18, 37, 53, 69, 87, 92, 117

Lund, Kimberly   16, 38

Pfeffer, Valerie   18, 60, 85, 90, 117

Rutten, Kristin   103, 124

Schenck, Alisa   35, 53

Thompson, Jessica Bree   20-21, 39, 85, 102, 118, 134-135

Truman, Stacey   15, 24, 76

Also available...

Real Life Scrapbooking Weekly Challenges - Scrapbook the real substance of your life ... those everyday moments that we can so easily forget to document but that become our fondest, most meaningful memories several years down the road. Each edition includes a complete year's worth of Weekly Challenges, including journaling prompts, sample layouts and more. Several versions available, including Kindle and Nook.

Baby's First Year Memory Logbook - The perfect tool for capturing baby's first year of life, this modern take on the traditional baby book is packed with opportunities to capture every one of those precious memories. Use it as a place to jot down notes and collect memorabilia for later scrapbooking ... or let it be your primary memory book. The book has been designed to work well whichever method you prefer.

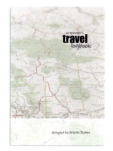

Scrapbooker's Travel Logbook - Log your trip & vacation memories with this shoulder bag-sized journal created with the scrapbooker in mind. Includes sections to record pre-, during & post-trip highlights. Ample room for journaling or sketching, plus room to log photos taken, summarize trip favorites, and more. Coordinating digital layered template album also available.

List My Life - Capture the details of your life through 100 open-ended lists, such as "lessons learned," "movies viewed," "challenges faced," "instruments played," "states visited," and "role models admired," just to name a few. There's even a handful of empty pages at the back for you to add your own unique lists. A great tool for capturing memories and the perfect springboard for scrapbook pages, if that's your interest.

Status Updated - A fun and easy way to preserve your favorite status updates from Twitter, Facebook or other social networking sites in a more permanent format. By taking just a few minutes each day, week, month ... whatever fits your lifestyle ... to transfer your updates to this book, you will be creating a lasting record of your everyday life that you and your family will be sure to treasure in the years to come.

www.CreativeOutletPublishing.com

CPSIA information can be obtained
at www.ICGtesting.com
Printed in the USA
LVIC061429140513
333779LV00006B